W9-BAG-469

Grades 3–6

# Teaching Comprehension With
# Nonfiction Read Alouds

## 12 Lessons For Using Newspapers, Magazines, and Other Nonfiction Texts To Build Key Comprehension Skills

### Dawn Little

**SCHOLASTIC**

New York • Toronto • London • Auckland • Sydney
Mexico City • New Delhi • Hong Kong • Buenos Aires

## Dedication

This book is dedicated to my husband and C & C, who each teach me new things every day. And to my mother, my first teacher, who continues to inspire me daily.

## Acknowledgements

I would like to thank Virginia Dooley and Sarah Glasscock for their amazing support and guidance through this process. My colleagues have inspired me through the years to constantly stay on top of my game: Toni Byrd, Bobbi Laydon, Somer Givens, and Julyna Martinez. Without the support and encouragement of my friend and colleague, Ramona Howard-Turner, this book would still be a dream. And last but not least, to the students who have walked through my classroom door through the years, it is because of each of you that my passion for teaching thrives!

Cover design by Jorge J. Namerow

Cover images: teacher: Morgan Lane Photography/Shutterstock® Images; others: Photodisc

Interior design by Holly Grundon

Editor: Sarah Glasscock

Copy Editor: Shelley Griffin

ISBN-13: 978-0-545-08743-8

ISBN-10: 0-545-08743-0

Copyright © 2010 Dawn Little

# Contents

# Introduction

If you were to sit in on any elementary classroom across the country, at some point in the day you would be likely to see a read aloud. Teachers in the lower grades often call it "story time." Teachers in the upper grades typically read a chapter from a novel. No matter what kind of text is read, however, being read to should be an integral part of every child's day. In fact, two decades ago in *Becoming a Nation of Readers* (Anderson, Hiebert, Scott, & Wilkinson, 1985) reading aloud was called "the single most important activity for building the knowledge required for eventual success in reading" (p. 23).

As teachers, we're all familiar with the importance of reading aloud. I hope that most of us take a few minutes each day to read to our students. We may read aloud a picture book to tie into a lesson or a novel that might be just over the reading level of our students. Being read to enables students to experience the pleasure that comes with escaping into the depths of a book. It provides a chance for students to relax and listen to a story or interesting piece of information. They don't have to worry about decoding the words or how fluent their reading is. And they almost always comprehend what they're hearing.

In my classroom, I found that while reading aloud is wonderful in and of itself, a read aloud can also be a useful teaching tool. You can use it as a discussion starter for a social studies topic, as an introduction to a new unit, or as a model for reading and writing strategies. The most important feature of read alouds in the classroom, however, is that they're interactive. The lessons in this book provide students with the opportunity to first reflect on the strategy presented in the read aloud; then practice using it in guided-reading groups, in pairs, and independently with the aid of graphic organizers; and finally to extend beyond the lessons, internalizing the newly learned strategies as they read and work on their own. These three stages elevate the read aloud to an instructional tool that helps students increase their ability to comprehend texts.

## Why Read Nonfiction Aloud?

A read aloud is a wonderful instructional tool for several reasons. First, it can be easily integrated into the curriculum. Typically, we teachers tend to read fictional pieces to our students, but a whole range of possibilities opens up if we begin to link reading aloud to the content areas of science, social studies, and math. Secondly, a read aloud can be used as an instructional springboard for discussions, as well as a tool for modeling reading strategies. You may already use a fiction read aloud along with a think-aloud to teach students about reading and writing strategies. Reading aloud nonfiction provides a natural transition to studying the genres of nonfiction in the classroom. Just as we want to provide mentor texts for students when they are reading and writing fiction, we should do the same with nonfiction. Most important though, a read aloud provides an opportunity for students to just listen to what language sounds like. As Patricia L. Scharer and her colleagues noted, "You can think of reading aloud as providing students with a massive infusion of comprehensible written language. In every way but decoding the words, listeners process texts that they hear read aloud" (Scharer, Pinnell, Lyons, & Fountas, 2005, p. 25; Fountas & Pinnell, 2005). Reading aloud nonfiction text gives us the opportunity to teach students about the language of nonfiction texts and how it differs from fictional texts. Listening to nonfiction allows students to process the material in a way that might not be available to them if the text weren't read aloud.

Reading aloud nonfiction in the classroom is an "efficient way for students to expand their vocabulary and concepts and share and understand texts" (Scharer et al., 2005, p. 25). I hope this book becomes a resource to help you plan, incorporate, and sustain reading aloud nonfiction in your classroom, helping you create a class full of engaged, motivated, interactive thinkers and readers.

Reading nonfiction aloud helps build students' fluency, vocabulary, background knowledge, and comprehension. What's more, as any teacher who regularly reads aloud knows, being read to motivates students to read on their own. Since nonfiction makes up approximately 85 percent of the reading done in middle school, high school, and adult daily life (Snowball, 1995), it is imperative that we introduce and encourage the reading of nonfiction texts at a young age. The ability to read and comprehend nonfiction, therefore, becomes important as children move through school. However, because nonfiction text differs so greatly from fiction text, many students struggle with comprehension.

The nonfiction read aloud can serve as an intermediate step as students ease their way into independently reading nonfiction. By reading aloud nonfiction, we are providing an opportunity for students to hear what it sounds like. We are building their background knowledge on a subject as well as their content vocabulary. We are enabling them to see how nonfiction is read, not necessarily from cover to cover, but often in bits and pieces. Most important, reading aloud nonfiction allows us to teach students reading strategies that they will carry with them for the rest of their lives.

## Creating a Standards-Based Read Aloud

As I created these read-aloud lessons, I aimed to use standards that all states and districts would be expected to reach. Using the Mid-continent Research for Education and Learning (McREL) standards as my guide, I created these lessons to meet the needs of all learners.

The lessons in this book touch on almost all the strategies and skills in this standard, and a corresponding graphic organizer for each mini-lesson is included (see pages 66–77).

## How to Use This Book

This book is intended to provide a framework for reading aloud nonfiction in the middle grades classroom. It will help you determine how to use a read aloud as an instructional tool, providing a rationale for bringing both nonfiction and reading aloud into your room. I give examples showing how you can integrate reading nonfiction aloud into your social studies, science, math, and language arts curriculums. I discuss ways to make the read aloud interactive, fully including your students in the process to enhance their comprehension of nonfiction text. I offer mini-lessons to teach reading strategies, such as text features, vocabulary, visualization, making inferences, and more. For each lesson, I tell what materials you'll need and suggest appropriate high-quality nonfiction texts based on the strategy being taught. I suggest ideas for differentiating the lessons and show how to move beyond the read aloud also by examining ways to reflect on the reading and extend the learning. Finally, I discuss how to assess your students' understanding of the reading.

This book will guide you as you set up a nonfiction read-aloud framework in your classroom. I encourage you not to view nonfiction read alouds as an "addition" to your already crowded curriculum; instead, they can be easily integrated into your daily language arts, math, science, or social studies blocks. So sit back, relax, and continue reading. You'll learn how to integrate nonfiction into your curriculum in a fun and effective way, and hopefully, you will reenergize your teaching in the process.

# chapter 1

# Getting Started With Nonfiction Read Alouds

> We read to children for all the same reasons we talk with children: to reassure, to entertain, to bond, to inform or explain, to arouse curiosity, to inspire.

**—Jim Trelease**

(from *The Read-Aloud Handbook*, page 4)

## What Is an Interactive Read Aloud?

An interactive read aloud involves students in the act of reading aloud. Sure, we could simply read aloud a nonfiction text to our students and hope they pick up on the important information we want them to receive, but why not invite them to join us on the journey? Allowing students to take part in the read aloud empowers them to make the reading their own. Each child is going to walk away with something different from the text. Yet by transforming a read aloud into an interactive lesson, we are providing our students with the opportunity to learn specific skills and strategies and to read with purpose.

An interactive read aloud consists of three major components: (1) the think-aloud, (2) the skill or strategy you're going to teach, and (3) student involvement. Presenting an interactive read aloud takes careful planning. You must consider the skill or strategy you want to teach and how best to model it using a think-aloud. Involving students is the crucial component. You can do this by providing students with opportunities to share their thinking as they listen to the text being read. Partner sharing is one simple way to do this, and many of the lessons in this book incorporate this sharing activity. It only takes a few minutes and allows students to gather new information and clarify their own thinking. Finally, you must give students time to reflect on the skill or strategy independently.

## The Purpose of the Interactive Read Aloud

One of the most important purposes of an interactive read aloud is modeling what good readers do. They do the following:

◆ Activate their prior knowledge before they read

◆ Ask questions as they read

◆ Make connections to what they read

◆ Make predictions about what they read

◆ Determine the importance of what they read

◆ Make inferences about what they read

◆ Summarize and synthesize what they read

◆ Use text features to help determine what the text is about

◆ Determine ways to understand unknown vocabulary

An interactive read aloud provides an opportunity for teachers to do the following:

◆ Model what good readers do

◆ Create meaningful and enjoyable reading experiences

◆ Model what good discussions about texts look like

◆ Allow students to process texts that might be too difficult for them

◆ Model fluent, thoughtful reading

◆ Engage readers in thoughtful reading and discussion of texts

◆ Create a community of readers who are enthusiastic about and engaged by nonfiction texts

Most of all, we want students to be able to transfer their knowledge of a skill or strategy to their own independent reading.

# Embedding the Think-Aloud Strategy

Reading aloud is not simply reading a book out loud. Although at times we may just want to read aloud for the simple pleasure of sharing a book, a read aloud is a perfect opportunity to show students how thinking as they read helps them understand the text better. This is where a think-aloud comes in. Teachers must model what good readers do. Embedding a think-aloud into a read aloud creates an instructionally sound practice.

## What Is a Think-Aloud?

A think-aloud (Harvey & Goudvis, 2007; Davey, 1983) is an activity in which you share your thoughts with students, showing how you construct meaning, out loud as you read aloud. We are always thinking as we read, but as accomplished readers, we probably aren't even aware of it. More than likely it has become an innate part of our reading process, but we want to show students that thinking is an integral part of reading. As you're reading aloud, you may, for instance, stop and wonder aloud what will happen next. You may make an inference out loud or make a connection to the text. By sharing your thoughts with students, you are showing them what thinking while reading looks like.

Since thinking aloud is an instructional tool, it is important to demonstrate to students when you are doing so. You might stop and say, "Hmm" before you think aloud. You might put the book down and then think aloud. You could also just explicitly state for your students that you are thinking aloud. They need to see how the thinking process works and how it is different from the reading process.

I define the reading process as the physical act of reading. The reading process consists of decoding the text. The thinking process is the comprehension of what is read, the understanding of the meaning of the words on the page. Therefore, the thinking process encompasses how we think when we read, what strategies we use to help us understand the text.

# Instructional Read-Aloud Model

Reading aloud any text provides the opportunity to create a classroom full of engaged listeners as well as readers. You want your read aloud to be interactive, to have purpose. You shouldn't think of it as filler or as an addition to an already full day. A read aloud is an instructional tool that can be utilized in a number of ways in the course of a day. The most instructionally sound way is to determine how best to use a read aloud to match your curriculum. Are you beginning a new unit in science? Are your students having trouble understanding graphing in math? Do they need more background information on Colonial America? Would they benefit from learning about the background of an author whose book they are about to read?

A well-planned and well-rehearsed read aloud can have implications beyond our classrooms. A read aloud provides an opportunity for students to hear what language sounds like. An interactive read aloud is all about listening comprehension (Harvey & Goudvis, 2007). It builds vocabulary. Students' comprehension increases. However, since the read aloud is an instructional tool, we must think about what it takes to make a read-aloud instructionally sound. In particular, what should a nonfiction read aloud look like? Below is an example of an instructional model that I've used in my classroom to read aloud both fiction and nonfiction. The model takes you through the steps of a read aloud, beginning with choosing the texts and ending with reflection and assessment.

## Planning the Lesson

An instructional read aloud is only as good as the text you choose and the lesson you create. The read aloud will only work if you read the text ahead of time and know where you'll make your instructional points.

It typically helps to begin with the strategy you have in mind. What do you want your students to get out of the lesson? What strategy do you want them to learn? How do you plan to use the text to get the lesson across? How will you assess your students? Once you have your goals in mind, it is time to choose the text.

Sometimes you can work in the opposite direction. You may already have a text in mind that you would like to read aloud to your students. If that's the case, read through the text to see what instructional points you can make using it as an illustration. You'll find a Nonfiction Read-Aloud Planning Sheet on page 65 that will help you do this.

## Choosing Texts

We need to be intentional in our text choices. Each time we choose to read aloud, we need to be sure we know what lesson we want our students to receive. Do we want to teach them how to make connections? Perhaps we want them to learn how to make inferences. Our goal could be as simple as teaching the features of nonfiction text. Whatever the lesson is, we need to be picky in our text choices. Choose high-quality texts that work best with the strategy or lesson you want to teach.

In *Wondrous Words* (1999), Katie Wood Ray discusses the idea of touchstone texts. These are books we know so well that we can pick and choose what instructional lessons to create from them. Planning a lesson becomes much easier if you already know the text. Ideally, some of your touchstone texts will be books that lend themselves to two or three different lessons. For example, I have used *When I Was Young in the Mountains* by Cynthia Rylant to teach lessons on brainstorming writing topics, creating moving endings, and making connections.

You may already have a trove of touchstone fiction texts in your classroom. I also suggest finding high-quality nonfiction texts that you come to know and love as well. (See Chapter 3 for more information on finding nonfiction texts to use for classroom read-aloud lessons.) One important point to remember as you're selecting nonfiction material: you don't have to read the text from cover to cover! In fact, you want to identify the part of the text that best fits your needs and read only that section. Or, you may want to use only the text features in the selection to help you convey your lesson.

## Before and During the Read Aloud

In order to be prepared during the read aloud, you need to plan ahead. What instructional points do you intend to make? Mark them in the text *prior to reading it aloud*. As you read aloud, stop at the places you've noted and think aloud about what you've noticed and any questions you might have. This is where you will introduce and model the reading strategy. Using the think-aloud strategy to explicitly talk about our thinking as we read helps us bring students along on the journey. Point out to your students that you are modeling for them what good readers do. Explain to students that until we train our brains to automatically use strategies as we read, it is helpful to mark our thinking as we read. Sticky notes are the easiest way to do this.

## After the Read Aloud

Once you've shared the new reading strategy with students, provide time for them to reflect on it. Over the course of several sessions, give students time to talk with their classmates about the strategy as well as time to reflect on their own about how the strategy will help them become better readers. In addition, tie the strategy lesson into your guided-reading lessons. Provide follow-up activities to extend students' learning. And finally, determine how you will assess your students and how the assessments will drive your future instruction.

### Reflection and Assessment

Since our goal is to use the read aloud as an instructional tool, we want to use it to teach students how to apply specific strategies and how these strategies will help them as readers and thinkers. Yet if we are always reading aloud, how will we ever know what our students are thinking? You want to begin to gradually release control of the read aloud to your students and have them practice using these strategies in groups or with partners. The goal is to get them to a point where they're using comprehension strategies as they read independently.

Providing a reflection component to the read-aloud model accomplishes two things. First, it allows students to process what they have heard and, hopefully, learned. Second, it gives you the opportunity to see which students are actively interacting with the text and the strategies that you've taught. Essentially, it provides a formative assessment piece.

A reflection component is the quickest and easiest way to assess a read aloud. Other useful tools for assessing your students include conferences, a Nonfiction Read-Aloud Comprehension Record, anecdotal records, and activities completed beyond the lesson. Information on these tools appears on pages 62–64. Most can be used informally to provide you with a more comprehensive look at your students' strategy acquisition.

# Differentiation

As our classrooms become increasingly diverse, the needs of our students become more wide ranging as well. Students struggle with reading for a variety of reasons. In order to make our classrooms open to all learners, we must be prepared to teach students of all abilities. This means we need to differentiate our instruction.

An interactive read aloud is one way to differentiate. First, students aren't embarrassed by having to try to read a text that is not at their independent level. Second, an interactive read aloud provides an opportunity for students to discuss the text with peers, which allows at-risk students to learn information that they may not have understood themselves from others. Two groups of students in particular benefit greatly from the differentiation afforded by reading aloud in the classroom: English language learners (ELLs) and reluctant readers.

## English Language Learners

English language learners (ELLs) come from various social, economic, and cultural backgrounds and with differing ability levels. So when differentiating for ELL students, we need first to determine what their needs are. Some ELLs learn best when we help to activate their prior knowledge: presenting vocabulary ahead of time, providing role-playing activities, encouraging opportunities for visualization, and by using graphic organizers. In addition, it is helpful for ELLs to work in cooperative groups to learn from others.

Look for opportunities to read aloud texts about ELLs' native cultures. This presents those students with the chance to be the experts and share their background knowledge about a topic. Essentially, it allows your ELL students to feel successful.

Reading aloud is a perfect opportunity to differentiate for ELL students and model what good reading sounds like. ELL students are able to listen to the nuances of a voice, the cadence of the text. They are able to hear what fluent reading sounds like. Their comprehension of the text is better because it is not complicated by a lack of fluency. In addition, an interactive read aloud uses graphic organizers, cooperative learning, and reading comprehension strategies; all are great models for ELL students.

## Reluctant Readers

Students may be reluctant to read for a number of different reasons: they don't identify themselves as readers, they don't find the value in reading, or they may just lack a general interest in reading. Whatever the reason, it is imperative that we reach out to these students and pull them back in and engage them. Motivation is the key to reaching these learners. Therefore, we have to become detectives (add that to our ever-growing list of roles in the classroom!) and determine what topics excite our reluctant readers.

Nonfiction is usually a great motivator for reluctant readers. Confer with these students and determine what their likes and dislikes are and then cater to their interests. If you have a reluctant reader who enjoys historical topics, determine which topics are his favorites and find books about them. When you read aloud a book on a reluctant learner's favorite topic, you are signaling to that student that his interests are important to you, and that reading is important. Reading aloud a book that engages your reluctant readers is the quickest way to reengage them.

## Scaffolding Instruction to Create Strong, Independent Readers

If we want our students to become strategic, lifelong, motivated, and engaged readers, then we must model those characteristics ourselves. We must show our students that reading is important. We must demonstrate how and why we use strategies when we read. We must express reasons for reading nonfiction, both explicitly and implicitly.

It is our role as teachers to show appropriate models of what we expect our students to accomplish. If we want our students to read nonfiction, they need to see us reading nonfiction. Teachers who model strategies and foster discussion know that students' command of strategies gets better as they practice using them (Ketch, 2005). To that end, here is a three-step scaffolding process I follow when setting up nonfiction read alouds in my classroom:

**1.** *Modeled: I model what I expect from my students. Students need explicit instruction in how they are to read nonfiction.*

**2.** *Guided: I guide my students to help them meet or exceed my expectations. I provide plenty of time to practice reading strategies with nonfiction, both in guided-reading groups as well as with partners.*

**3.** *Independent: I provide students with the opportunity to succeed on their own and to strategically read nonfiction independently.*

This process is meant to help you plan and integrate reading aloud nonfiction in your own classroom in a gradual-release model. By providing scaffolding for students, you are providing plenty of opportunities for them to succeed. The lessons in Chapter 2 are set up to guide you through this three-step process. They are designed to help you model for your students, offer some guidance through the process, and then allow them to practice on their own.

In order for our students to become lifelong readers of nonfiction text, we must introduce them to nonfiction earlier in their school career. We must provide explicit, strategic instruction to help them become cognitive readers. And we need to create opportunities for our students to interact with nonfiction texts and their peers in an environment where they feel free to take risks.

# Reading Aloud Across the Curriculum

Reading aloud nonfiction provides many cross-curricular instructional opportunities. In the table on page 15, you will find ways that reading aloud nonfiction can support your instruction.

# Scheduling a Read Aloud

Initially, a strategy-based read-aloud lesson should occur over several days and last up to two weeks. Session 1, the read aloud and model lesson, takes about 45 minutes and should occur on one day. Think about when the read aloud will best fit into your day. Are you using a text that ties into your math, science, or social studies curriculum? Perhaps you want to begin that class session by modeling the strategy with a related read aloud.

Session 2, the subsequent guided reading and independent work, should occur over a span of several days and for up to two weeks following the original model lesson. Each group meeting should last about 20 minutes. These lessons can take place during your scheduled guided-reading time or your general language arts time.

# The Components of a Strategy Lesson

I call each mini-lesson a strategy lesson, because one of the goals when reading aloud nonfiction is to model a reading comprehension strategy for students.

The mini-lessons are intended to be taught to the whole class as a model lesson. Beyond that, they contain components for using guided practice in groups of four to six students and for independent work with the strategy. I recommend that you choose different texts to continue with the guided and student practice sessions. Each of the 12 lessons in Chapter 2 adheres to the same general structure discussed below.

## Benchmark

Each lesson meets a benchmark of Standard 7 of the McREL standards (see page 6 for the standard and its benchmarks).

## Strategy

Each lesson introduces a reading strategy. The lessons appear in the order they should be taught because the strategies should build on one another. For example, in order for students to be able to use text features to activate their prior knowledge, they need to know what text features are. Therefore, the text feature lesson comes before the lesson on activating prior knowledge.

## Ways Reading Aloud Nonfiction Can Support Instruction

| | |
|---|---|
| **Language Arts** | Read aloud the biography of an author the class is studying. |
| | Read background information on a topic covered in a fiction text the class is reading. |
| | **Examples:** Read *How I Came to Be a Writer* by Phyllis Reynolds Naylor prior to reading *Shiloh*.<br><br>Read background information on boys' detention centers prior to reading *Holes* by Louis Sachar. |
| **Math** | Provide background information on the topic you are studying (i.e., the history of money). |
| | Supplement a lesson on graphing. |
| | **Examples:** *From Seashells to Smart Cards* by Ernestine Giesecke is a good resource to use when studying money.<br><br>*USA Today* is a great source for graphs. |
| **Science** | Provide a vocabulary lesson prior to starting a new topic. |
| | Activate prior knowledge prior to starting a new unit. |
| | **Examples:** Use an article from *Science World* to highlight vocabulary as well as activate prior knowledge before a unit (see lesson on page 43).<br><br>*Ranger Rick* is also a good resource for science topics. |
| **Social Studies** | Use a read aloud to analyze a historical document. |
| | Read aloud historical letters for students to analyze. |
| | **Examples:** Analyze the preamble of the Declaration of Independence. Infer the meaning of the vocabulary.<br><br>Determine the importance of text found in historical letters, such as those in *The Letters of John and Abigail Adams* by Frank Shuffelton. |
| **Music** | Provide an in-depth study of musicians in history; read aloud biographies and other informative texts about the musicians. |
| | Delve into the history of music or specific instruments. |
| | **Examples:** *Lives of the Musicians* by Kathleen Krull creates 16 snapshot biographies of important people in musical history.<br><br>*Story of the Orchestra* by Robert Levine provides information about composers, their music, and historical events. |
| **Art** | Analyze an artist's work through his or her biography/autobiography. |
| | Study a specific time period in art. |
| | **Examples:** *Who Was Leonardo da Vinci?* by Roberta Edwards gives information on da Vinci's background, artwork, and inventions. |
| **Physical Education** | Read aloud biographies of various sports stars and the history of a specific sport. |
| | Read aloud texts on health and physical fitness. |
| | **Examples:** Read *Lance Armstrong: A Biography* by Bill Gutman and ask students to make connections.<br><br>Read *Bicycling* by Julie S. Bach and have students determine important ideas from the text. |

Once a lesson has been taught, you should continue to revisit the strategy, even as you begin to teach new ones. I suggest working on one strategy for a two-week period before adding a new one. During that time, you can reinforce the strategy using different texts, work on it in guided-reading groups, and encourage students to use the strategy independently. I recommend that you revisit a previously taught strategy at least once a week. You can use the Revisiting Strategy Sessions chart on page 17 as a guide.

You can build on the lessons in this book by gradually releasing responsibility to students, working on the same strategy in guided reading, and then when students are confident enough, allowing them to work on the strategy independently. Eventually, the goal is for students to use the strategies on their own without the support of sticky notes or graphic organizers.

## Objective

The objective states which strategy students will know and be able to use at the completion of the lesson.

## Differentiation Tips

When appropriate, I offer ways to differentiate the activity for ELLs or reluctant readers.

## Essential Literacy Question

Each strategy lesson includes one or more Essential Literacy Questions (ELQ). Prior to a lesson, I post at least one ELQ on the board or chart paper. The ELQ relates to the lesson and can be used to activate students' prior knowledge before the lesson or to prompt reflection at the end of the model lesson. Additionally, the ELQs serve as a guide to help you to think about what your lesson should include. Students should be able to answer one or more of the ELQs at the completion of your model lesson (even if they don't do it as part of reflection). If students have difficulty answering the question(s), you know that you must reinforce the strategy and model again.

## Vocabulary Preview

Prior to reading nonfiction text, it is helpful to preview vocabulary words that you expect to be difficult for students. Building students' vocabulary will help them understand the text as it's read. Lessons 1–3 do not include vocabulary previews because students are either learning about text structures, text features, or author's purpose and are not necessarily reading text in which they will need to know vocabulary. Lesson 4 is a vocabulary lesson, and the strategy within that lesson can be used to preview vocabulary in subsequent lessons. Other ways to preview vocabulary appear on page 18.

| | Revisiting Strategy Sessions | |
|---|---|---|
| Week | Strategy | Revisit |
| 1 | Using Text Structures | |
| 2 | Using Text Structures | |
| 3 | Using Text Features | |
| 4 | Using Text Features | Using Text Structures |
| 5 | Determining Author's Purpose | Using Text Features |
| 6 | Determining Author's Purpose | Using Text Structures |
| 7 | Making Vocabulary Inferences | Determining Author's Purpose |
| 8 | Making Vocabulary Inferences | Using Text Features |
| 9 | Activating Prior Knowledge | Making Vocabulary Inferences |
| 10 | Activating Prior Knowledge | Determining Author's Purpose |
| 11 | Making Connections | Activating Prior Knowledge |
| 12 | Making Connections | Making Vocabulary Inferences |
| 13 | Asking Questions | Making Connections |
| 14 | Asking Questions | Activating Prior Knowledge |
| 15 | Making Predictions | Asking Questions |
| 16 | Making Predictions | Making Connections |
| 17 | Determining Important Ideas | Making Predictions |
| 18 | Determining Important Ideas | Asking Questions |
| 19 | Visualization | Determining Important Ideas |
| 20 | Visualization | Making Predictions |
| 21 | Making Inferences | Visualization |
| 22 | Making Inferences | Determining Important Ideas |
| 23 | Summarizing Text | Making Inferences |
| 24 | Summarizing Text | Visualization |
| 25 | | Summarizing Text |
| 26 | | Making Inferences |
| 27 | | Summarizing Text |
| Beyond | | |

## Ways to Preview Vocabulary

**Picture Talk:** Before beginning a lesson on a new topic, locate or create pictures that illustrate vocabulary words necessary for an understanding of the topic. Post the pictures on a sheet of chart paper and ask students what they already know about the pictures. On the chart paper next to the pictures, write what students share. Guide them to the correct vocabulary word for each picture.

**Sentence Strip Vocabulary**: Prior to reading aloud a piece of text, choose three or four vocabulary words whose meanings students should be able to comprehend by the context of the text. Write the sentence or sentences on sentence strips and post them. Help students use the context of the sentence to discover the meaning of the words.

**Word Splash**: A word splash is a motivational activity that provides a purpose for reading while previewing vocabulary words. Prior to reading about a new topic, write the topic in the middle of the page and "splash" seven to ten familiar and unfamiliar words from the text around it at various angles. Ask students to write one sentence for each word predicting what he or she thinks the text is going to be about. Read aloud the text and have students confirm their predictions.

## Vocabulary Notebooks

Vocabulary notebooks are a useful tool for students, especially when they are working with nonfiction texts. For instance, students can list new vocabulary words and their meanings in vocabulary notebooks. I don't recommend having students make a list of words and then look up the meanings in the dictionary. Instead, students can use their vocabulary notebooks to complete their vocabulary preview activities. Or, you can have students draw pictures of what the word means to them. This is a useful way for ELLs to learn new vocabulary as well.

## Text Choices

Since nonfiction comes in all different shapes and sizes, I tend to use the term "text" instead of "book." I find it is best to use short texts to practice a strategy and especially for reading aloud. Newspaper articles from *USA Today* or your local newspaper; articles from *Time for Kids*, *Scholastic News*, *Ranger Rick*, *National Geographic for Kids*, *Cobblestone*, and *Kids Discover* are just a few of the different types of nonfiction text that can be used as a read aloud.

## Preparation

Nonfiction read alouds require a few preparatory steps. For each lesson in this book, you'll need to make copies of a corresponding graphic organizer (see pages 66–77), as well as reproduce the organizer on a class-size chart. Students will need to have their Reflect and Revise notebooks (see page 20) and/or other notebooks handy. It is also helpful to have sticky notes available for student use.

## Activating Prior Knowledge

Before beginning a new unit in a content area, gather several books on the topic to display and/or read aloud to the class. When reading nonfiction texts, it is important to activate students' prior knowledge about the topic. This provides students with the opportunity to summon what they already know about the topic, which aids their comprehension of the text. In addition to activating prior knowledge about the content, it is also important to activate prior knowledge of the strategy. Each lesson includes one activity that activates prior knowledge, and the strategy within it can also be used to activate prior knowledge in subsequent lessons.

## Ways to Activate Prior Knowledge

**K-W-L:** The K-W-L chart (Harvey, 1998; Ogle, 1986) is a three-column chart used to activate students' prior knowledge. It is headed "What I Know," "What I Want to Know," and "What I Learned." Prior to hearing a read aloud, students fill out what they already know about the topic and what they want to know. After reading, students fill out what they learned. The K-W-L chart should be used only to activate and build on students' prior knowledge. In other words, K-W-L charts should be used judiciously. Often, we become too comfortable with one tool and overuse it. This seems to be especially true for the K-W-L. The K-W-L does make it easy for teachers and students to activate prior knowledge, but when we use it all the time, it loses its validity.

**Feature Walk**: Prior to reading a nonfiction text, allow students to take a feature walk. Students page through the text, look at the pictures or photographs, and read the captions and other bits of information, but they do not read the body of the text. Then they write down any questions they have that they think might be answered in the body of the text. After reading, students go back and see if their questions were answered.

**Anticipation Guide**: An anticipation guide (Smith, 1978) consists of seven to ten statements that are either taken from the text or that simply concern its topic and which may or may not be true. The statements are written in the center of the page, with two columns labeled "True" and "False" to the left of the statements and two more "True" and "False" columns to the right. Before the read aloud, students mark whether they think the statements are true or false in one column. Once the text has been read, students return to the statements and again mark whether they consider them true or false in the other column. After the guides have been completed, use them to lead a discussion. Anticipation guides and the discussions they stimulate help students clear up any misinformation they may have about a topic.

## Lesson Introduction

The lesson introduction is the place in the lesson in which you explicitly state to students the strategy you are going to model and the purpose behind it.

## Conducting the Lesson

When you conduct the lesson, you are modeling the strategy for students. During this time, you may use texts, graphic organizers, sticky notes, and other materials to explicitly model for students the strategy lesson.

## Reflection

Reflection is an important aspect to any lesson. Without reflection, we are not aware of what our students have really learned, or more important, what they did not learn. Reflections can be oral or written but should occur after the model lesson and prior to guided reading or student practice. Reflection can help you determine your guided-reading groups as this process informs you of what your students have learned and which ones need reinforcement. Below are a few ways you can have your students reflect after a read aloud.

**Talk-Aloud:** A talk-aloud is an opportunity for students to discuss text that has been read aloud to them. Talk-aloud can be informal: having students turn and talk to the person next to them about what they heard and learned or giving students a question to discuss as they share responses and ideas. A talk-aloud provides students the opportunity to process what they have heard.

**Reflect and Revise Notebooks:** These notebooks are different from reading journals because students are expected and encouraged to make changes to their original reflections on their reading. I use these notebooks in almost every lesson to help students activate their prior knowledge and to reflect on what they learned after hearing a read aloud. This is a way for students to synthesize their thinking throughout the year. As they continue to learn more about a topic, strategy, or lesson, they are asked to revise their thinking.

**Reading Journals:** I consider reading journals a place for students to take independent notes about their texts in literature circles and as a place to complete other literary activities. These journals are different from Reflect and Revise notebooks because once students have written in these, they are not expected to revise their writing.

## Guided Practice

After modeling a strategy with a read aloud, continue to work with it in guided-reading groups. You can modify the lesson by using different texts with the same lesson or create similar strategy lessons to allow students time to practice using the strategy with your guidance. Guided practice typically occurs in small groups. This allows you to work with about four to six students and really concentrate on providing them with explicit instruction related to the strategy. This practice usually lasts about 15 to 20 minutes.

## Independent Practice

Once students have had ample time to practice using the strategy with your guidance, provide them with opportunities to use the strategy in small groups, with partners, or independently. They may still need to use their graphic organizer and sticky notes, but eventually, they should feel so confident using the strategy that it becomes second nature to them. The goal is to make students metacognitively aware of which strategies they are using when they read.

## Beyond the Lesson

Even after the formal lesson is over, learning continues. Students need to constantly work with the new strategy in order to master it. Beyond the Lesson activities are meant to allow time for students to use the newly learned strategy in other ways. They might work in a learning center with partners or independently.

———————

A nonfiction read aloud is an instructional tool that can help students build connections within content areas. Connecting nonfiction to what you are already teaching makes incorporating nonfiction read alouds into your day easier. If you utilize a nonfiction read aloud to model strategy instruction, you have an instructional device that can empower your teaching and engage your students.

# chapter 2

# Interactive Read Aloud:
# Strategy Lessons

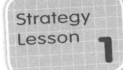

**Strategy Lesson 1**

## Identifying Different Nonfiction Text Structures

**McREL benchmark:** Understands structural patterns or organization in informational texts

**Strategy:** Using text structures

**Objective:** Students will be able to identify different text structures of nonfiction text.

---

### Essential Literacy Question (ELQ)

How does identifying a text's structure help you understand the text better?

### Text Choices

◆ a text that shows cause and effect

◆ a text that shows a problem and solution

◆ a text that shows question and answers

◆ a text that shows comparison and contrast

◆ a text that shows description

◆ a text that shows chronological order

**Differentiation Tip**

After you conduct the model lesson and subsequent guided-reading sessions, have ELLs work in cooperative groups with native-speaking students to determine various text structures.

### Preparation

◆ Review one piece of text for each of the major nonfiction text structures.

◆ Make overheads of the texts to share with students. (**Note:** Typically, we don't show text in a read aloud; however, in this instance, students must be able to see the text in order to understand the components of text structure.)

◆ Post the ELQ.

- ◆ Make a copy of the Structures of Text graphic organizer for each student and prepare a display copy.

- ◆ Students will need their Reflect and Revise notebooks.

- ◆ Gather the following materials: chart paper, markers, index cards, additional text choices for guided and independent practice.

Structures of Text, p. 66

## Session 1

**Activating Prior Knowledge:** Ask students to work in pairs to answer the following question in their Reflect and Revise notebooks: What do you know about nonfiction text structures? Ask students to record their answers in their notebooks. Discuss their responses as a class. Post their ideas on chart paper. Explain that today they are going to learn about text structures.

## Model Lesson

**Introduction:** *Text is written in various structures. This makes it easier for readers to understand what they're reading. Today I am going to model for you how to determine what type of text structure you're reading.* Post a chart with the six most common text structures: cause and effect, problem and solution, questions and answers, comparison and contrast, description, and chronological order, as well as some cue words for each of the text structures. *These are the six most common text structures and the cue words that will help you determine the type of text structure you're reading. As I read the texts today, I'm going to think aloud about what type of structure the text might have.*

| Cue Words to Help Identify Text Structures | |
|---|---|
| Cause and Effect | *as a result, because, therefore, caused by, led to* |
| Problem and Solution | *the issue, need to prevent, answer, response, to solve the problem* |
| Comparison and Contrast | *in contrast, instead, in comparison, the same as, difference, compared to* |
| Questions and Answers | A question is usually noted, and an answer follows. |
| Description | *for example, specifically, characteristics are, a description of* |
| Sequencing | *next, finally, afterward, following, before, after, to start with* |

**Conducting the Lesson:** Show students the display chart of the Structures of Text graphic organizer and then read aloud your selected text. As you read, stop and think aloud about the types of cue words you are encountering. You may want to underline or circle them. Think aloud about the specific words you are highlighting. Note how these cue words help you determine what the text structure may be. For example: *Hmm, I see the phrase, "as a result" so I'm going to underline that.* Continue to read aloud. *Now I see the word "because." This is beginning to make me think that the structure here is cause and effect.* Continue to read aloud. *Aha, now I see the word "therefore." I definitely think this piece is cause and effect. If I look back at my cue words chart, I can see that these words are cue words for a cause and effect text structure. But, I also see that there is a specific cause* [state it] *and a specific effect* [state it] *in this piece.* As you determine the text structure for each piece, write its title and structure on the Structures of Text display chart. This provides a classroom resource poster for students to use when they need guidance. Additionally, keep copies of the texts you read aloud to the class in a binder with a copy of the Structures of Text graphic organizer as a classroom resource book for students. As you model with other texts or you use different texts during guided reading, add those to the binder.

**Reflection:** Ask students to answer the ELQ in their Reflect and Revise notebooks. Tell students that they may revise their thinking as they learn more.

## Session 2

After the model lesson takes place, multiple guided practice sessions and individual student practice sessions should occur over a span of two weeks. In addition to the activities below, you may want to plan for extra activities based on your students' needs.

**Guided Practice:** Provide groups with texts that demonstrate various text structures. Ask them to determine which structure the text has and which cue words helped them to identify it. Have students record this information on their own individual Structures of Text graphic organizer with your guidance.

**Student Practice:** Give a group six short pieces of text and six index cards. Each index card should include a list of cue words that matches a text structure. Have students work together, reading each piece of text and determining its structure by using the cue-word cards as a guide. Then ask students to complete the Structures of Text graphic organizer on their own.

## Beyond the Lesson

1. Have students use the classroom resource poster and book for model texts when they are writing and aren't sure what its structure should be.

2. Create a learning center with various text structure examples. Stock it with Structures of Text organizers and provide an opportunity for students to determine which structures the examples show.

*Teaching Comprehension With Nonfiction Read Alouds*

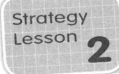
# Discovering Nonfiction Text Features

**McREL benchmark:** Uses the various parts of a book to locate information

**Strategy:** Using text features to better comprehend text

**Objective:** Students will be able to use text features to help them better understand a text.

## Essential Literacy Question (ELQ)

How do text features help you understand the text?

## Text Choices

◆ a big book, such as *Animal Senses* by Melvin Berger

◆ a nonfiction book with examples of a variety of text features, such as *Chimp Math* by Ann Whitehead Nagda and Cindy Bickel

## Differentiation Tip

Send pairs of students on a picture scavenger hunt to locate text features in nonfiction. Make copies of the most common text features (table of contents, bold and italicized words, photos, captions, illustrations, diagrams, glossary, and index) from a nonfiction text. Ask students to locate the text features based on the pictures.

## Preparation

◆ Prepare overheads of a variety of different text features. (**Note:** Typically, we don't show text in a read aloud; however, in this instance, students must be able to see the text in order to recognize and identify various text features.)

◆ Post the ELQ.

◆ Make a copy of the Nonfiction Text Features Checklist for each student and prepare a display copy.

◆ Students will need their Reflect and Revise notebooks.

◆ Gather the following materials: chart paper, markers.

Nonfiction Text Features Checklist, p. 67

## Session 1

**Activating Prior Knowledge:** Ask students what they think the noun *feature* means and to respond in their Reflect and Revise notebook. Post and discuss their responses.

## Model Lesson

**Introduction:** Gather the class in a group around you. If you can use a big book for this lesson, it will be easier for all to see the features you are highlighting. However, any text with a variety of text features will do. If you don't have an actual text to use as a model, use overheads of a variety of text features. As you begin the lesson say, *There are many differences between the genre of fiction and the genre of nonfiction. One difference is in the ways fiction and nonfiction are organized. Most nonfiction texts have specific structures and features. We've learned about the different text structures in nonfiction. Now we can use text features to help us read and understand nonfiction text. Today, I am going to show you a text that is full of nonfiction features.*

**Conducting the Lesson:** Open the text. Ask students what they notice. Guide them to discuss the text features you point out. Start at the table of contents. *What is one thing you notice that may be different from a work of fiction? Since nonfiction is informational text, authors make it easier for us to read by guiding us to the information. One way they do this is by creating a table of contents. A table of contents usually lists specific headings and tells us on which pages we can find information related to those headings.*

Turn the page. Ask students what they notice now. Guide them to notice headings. *Nonfiction texts often separate information into sections to make it easier to find the information we are looking for. In this section, you can learn about . . .* [Share with your students what they can learn about from the heading.] Ask students if they notice anything about the size of the text. *The heading is the largest text on the page. Why do you think that is?* Allow time for answers. *The heading needs to stand out so that the reader knows what the section is about. The main text on the page that gives us most of the information is smaller but still nice and big enough to read easily. The smallest text on the page is typically used for captions. Captions are bits of information that describe a picture.* Read a caption and discuss how it describes the picture it goes with.

Ask if anyone notices anything else. Point out a pronunciation key if there is one. Explain that sometimes nonfiction text uses words that are hard to pronounce. Discuss any other features or questions your students may have. Ask students if they notice any words that stand out. Explain that sometimes authors of nonfiction texts make words stand out by setting them in boldface or italics. This usually indicates that the word or words are important. To complete this lesson, turn to the back page and point out the index. Explain its purpose: It allows us to find information quickly by giving specific information and the page numbers where we can find the information.

*Teaching Comprehension With Nonfiction Read Alouds*

After completing this part of the lesson, post the display copy of the Nonfiction Text Features Checklist and ask students which types of text features were in the book you just explored. Record their responses on the chart. If necessary, go back into the text to locate the features again. Explain that while you found a few text features today, there are many more that weren't used in this text.

**Reflection:** Ask students to turn to the person next to them and complete an informal talk-aloud about the different nonfiction text features they learned about today. After allowing time for discussion, have them answer the ELQ in their Reflect and Revise notebook. Remind students that they may revise their thinking as they continue to learn about nonfiction text features.

## Session 2

After the model lesson takes place, multiple guided practice sessions and individual student practice sessions should occur over a span of two weeks. In addition to the activities below, you may want to plan for extra activities based on your students' needs.

**Guided Practice:** Continue working on text features with students in guided-reading groups. Ask students to locate specific text features in a selected text and discuss what the purpose of each feature might be. Have them record these text features on the Nonfiction Text Features Checklist.

**Student Practice:** Provide student pairs with their own nonfiction text (a trade book, a chapter in a textbook, a news magazine—tie it into your curriculum if you like) and allow them to look through the text to identify nonfiction features. As pairs skim and scan the text, they should complete the Nonfiction Text Features Checklist together.

## Beyond the Lesson

1. Ask students to create a list of nonfiction text features in their reading journals. They can keep a running list and add to it as they read independently and find new features.

2. When students write reports or share information in a written format, include a component that allows them to create visuals like the ones they might find in a nonfiction text. For example, they may want to draw a picture and add a caption. Or they might create a graph that will add to the reader's understanding.

# Determining the Author's Purpose

**McREL benchmark:** Uses reading skills and strategies to understand a variety of informational texts

**Strategy:** Determine the author's purpose in writing a nonfiction text

**Objective:** Students will be able to analyze various nonfiction texts to determine the author's purpose in writing each one.

## Essential Literacy Questions (ELQs)

**1.** Why do you think that authors write for different purposes?

**2.** How can you determine an author's purpose for writing a text?

## Text Choices

◆ a set of directions

◆ a series of jokes or riddles

◆ a series of questions and answers

◆ a short persuasive article

◆ a short informative news article

### Differentiation Tip

Provide students with several different pieces of text written for different purposes. Ask them to work in cooperative groups of four to six. Give key words or phrases and the author's purpose and have students locate the phrases in the appropriate text to determine the author's purpose.

## Preparation

◆ Locate several short pieces of text written for a variety of reasons and determine the author's purpose.

◆ Post the ELQs.

◆ Make a copy of the What Is the Author's Purpose? graphic organizer for each student and prepare a display copy.

What Is the Author's Purpose?, p. 68

*Teaching Comprehension With Nonfiction Read Alouds*

- Students will need their Reflect and Revise notebooks.
- Gather the following materials: chart paper, markers.

## Session 1

**Activating Prior Knowledge:** Ask students to answer the first ELQ in their Reflect and Revise notebooks: Why do you think that authors write for different purposes? Discuss their answers. Remind students that they may want to revise their answers as they learn more about writing for different purposes.

## Model Lesson

**Introduction:** *Authors write for many different reasons. Today, we are going to discover some of those reasons. They usually write a piece that fits into one of three categories: they write to inform, to persuade, or to entertain.*

**Conducting the Lesson:** Begin by reading aloud the various pieces of text you've gathered, one at a time. As you read, think aloud about the author's purpose: Is he or she writing to inform? To entertain? To persuade? Post the What Is the Author's Purpose? display chart you prepared. As you read each piece of text and determine its purpose, list the title and author under the correct category on the chart. Give specific information to students explaining why you chose the purpose you did, such as the following: *I like how the author told me what the problem was [share examples], gave me solutions to the problem [share examples], and then used specific persuasive language [share examples] to ask me to help. Therefore, I am going to put this piece under "Write to Persuade" on the What Is the Author's Purpose? chart.* Tell students: *As you read other pieces throughout the year, you should be able to determine what the author's purpose is for writing. When you do, add the title of the piece and the author's name to the class chart.* Anything you read aloud to the class should be added to the chart as well. Keep the chart posted in the classroom throughout the year. The chart then serves as a classroom resource. When students need mentor texts to help them determine their purpose as an author, they can use those on the chart to guide them.

    **Note:** Be sure to check the chart periodically to make sure students are placing the texts in the right categories. When you find that a student may have placed a text in the wrong category, use it as a teachable moment. Ask why the student thought that the piece fit where he or she put it. Give specific language from the text to show why the piece should fit in a different category.

**Reflection:** Ask students to answer the second ELQ in their Reflect and Revise notebooks: How can you determine an author's purpose for writing a text? Remind them that they may want to revise their thinking as they continue to learn more about author's purpose.

## Session 2

After the model lesson takes place, multiple guided practice sessions and individual student practice sessions should occur over a span of two weeks. In addition to the activities below, you may want to plan for extra activities based on your students' needs.

**Guided Practice:** Hand out several pieces of text to students in guided-reading groups. Name one of the three author purposes and ask students to identify the texts that fall under that category. Students should be able to locate the key words or phrases that helped them identify the purpose. Distribute individual copies of the What Is the Author's Purpose? organizer and ask students to add one or two texts to it.

**Student Practice:** Give student pairs an opportunity to categorize different pieces of text by author's purpose. Provide individual copies of the What Is the Author's Purpose? organizer for each student to use and keep in their reading journals. This organizer allows students to keep their own running list of pieces they have read as they record authors' purposes.

## Beyond the Lesson

1. Have students use the What Is the Author's Purpose? display chart when they have a piece of writing to work on and they aren't sure what their purpose is going to be or if they need to turn to a mentor text to help them choose language specific to their purpose.

2. Tell students to read three pieces of text written for different purposes and then identify the words or phrases that helped them determine the author's purpose.

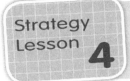

# Vocabulary Inferences

**McREL benchmark:** Draws conclusions and makes inferences based on explicit and implicit information in texts

**Strategy:** Making vocabulary inferences

**Objective:** Students will be able to make inferences to help them determine a word's meaning.

## Essential Literacy Question (ELQ)
How does inferring the meaning of a word help you understand the word in context?

## Text Choices
◆ periodical articles, such as "The First Lady's Confidant" in *Secrets of the Civil War* by U.S. News and World Report and "Meriwether and William—or Lewis and Clark" in *The New Nation* by Joy Hakim

### Differentiation Tip

Have students draw pictures to remind them of the meaning of the words they learn in this lesson. They can place their pictures in their vocabulary notebook.

## Preparation

◆ Review a short piece of text that you plan to read aloud. Determine which words you will need to preview for students to have a firm understanding of the text. **Note:** You will need to review a different periodical article or section in a textbook or trade book prior to guided practice and independent practice in order to determine the vocabulary to preview with students.

◆ Post the ELQ.

◆ Make a copy of the Inferring Vocabulary graphic organizer for each student and prepare a display copy. Write the words that need to be previewed on the organizer.

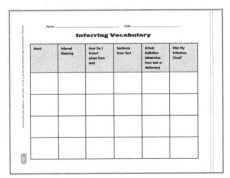
Inferring Vocabulary, p. 69

- Students will need their Reflect and Revise notebooks and their Vocabulary notebooks.

- Gather the following materials: chart paper, markers, dictionaries.

## Session 1

**Activating Prior Knowledge:** Ask students what they think the word *infer* means. Tell them to respond in their Reflect and Revise notebooks and then write the method that they used to determine the meaning. Discuss the meanings they produced and guide them to an accurate definition, if necessary.

## Model Lesson

**Introduction:** Prior to reading aloud the article, post the display chart of the Inferring Vocabulary organizer with the vocabulary words for preview. Explain to students that you are going to model how to make inferences to figure out unfamiliar words. *Today we are going to learn about a strategy that will help us determine the meaning of a word. Sometimes when we read nonfiction, we come across words that we don't understand. We will learn how to infer, or make inferences, to try to make sense of unfamiliar words. When we make inferences, we take our background knowledge and any clues we can find in the text to make an educated guess about something. Sometimes we can figure out if our inference is correct, but sometimes we are left wondering. This is because an inference is implied, so the answer is never directly stated in the text.*

**Conducting the Lesson:** Identify and discuss each vocabulary word posted on the organizer. Explain that you are going to read aloud the text and, as you come across an unfamiliar word, you will stop and infer its meaning based on your background knowledge and the clues in the text.

Begin reading aloud. As you come to each vocabulary word, stop and fill in the Inferring Vocabulary graphic organizer as you think aloud, but leave the Actual Definition column blank. Once you have finished the text, go back and fill in the actual definition for each word, using the dictionary if necessary. Many definitions may be determined by reading the text. Determine if the inference was close to the actual definition. If not, ask students to write these words and their actual definitions in their Vocabulary notebooks (see page 18). Reread the text aloud once students have a firm understanding of the meanings of the words.

**Reflection:** Have students complete the ELQ in their Reflect and Revise notebook: How does inferring the meaning of a word help you understand the word in context? Remind students that as they get used to the idea of inferring the meaning of words, they may want to return to this question and revise their answers.

## Session 2

After the model lesson takes place, multiple guided practice sessions and individual student practice sessions should occur over a span of two weeks. In addition to the activities below, you may want to plan for extra activities based on your students' needs.

**Guided Practice:** Provide students with a short article from a periodical or a section in a trade book or textbook. Using the Inferring Vocabulary organizer, work with a group to infer the meaning of vocabulary you pulled from the text. Model how to use the Inferring Vocabulary organizer with two or three words. Provide an opportunity for students to work on two or three more vocabulary words with a partner. Each pair should complete an organizer together.

**Student Practice:** Have students work in pairs to read a nonfiction text. As they come upon vocabulary words they don't know, encourage them to list the vocabulary and complete the Inferring Vocabulary graphic organizer together. Students should then reread the piece to determine if it makes sense once they have an understanding of the words.

## Beyond the Lesson

1. Create a learning center stocked with Inferring Vocabulary graphic organizers and short pieces of nonfiction text. Provide opportunities for students to read the text and complete the organizers.

2. Have students create an illustrated vocabulary concept wall. As students learn new vocabulary for a topic you are studying, encourage them to draw a picture of the concept and write a definition. Post the illustrations and definitions on the concept wall.

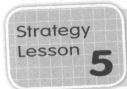

## Strategy Lesson 5: Activating Prior Knowledge by Asking Questions

**McREL benchmark:** Uses prior knowledge and experience to understand and respond to new information

**Strategy:** Activating prior knowledge by asking questions before reading

**Objective:** Students will be able to ask questions before reading to help determine what they already know about a topic.

### Essential Literacy Questions (ELQs)

**1.** How does asking questions help you activate your prior knowledge of the topic?

**2.** How does activating prior knowledge help you understand the text?

### Text Choices

◆ an article from a periodical, such as "Remembering Lincoln" by Brenda Iasevoli from *Time for Kids*

◆ a section of a trade book, such as *Butterflies* by David Bjerklie

### Vocabulary Preview:

Provide students with a list of words from the text that are essential to understanding it. Group students and ask them to draw a picture of one word as they understand it (make sure each group has a different word). Have the class share pictures and discuss meanings.

> ### Differentiation Tip
>
> Provide students with a short nonfiction text. Before students read the text, ask them to work in cooperative groups of four to six to activate their prior knowledge of the topic of the text. Present several topics based on the text and have students create questions that can be categorized within the topics.

### Preparation

◆ Review a short text that has plenty of text features to read aloud. If you like, tie the text into your curriculum. Note particular places you want to draw students' attention to—think about the types of questions they might ask.

- Post the ELQs.

- Make a copy of the Sticky Questions graphic organizer for each student and prepare a display copy.

- Gather the following materials: chart paper, markers, and 3-inch x 3-inch sticky notes.

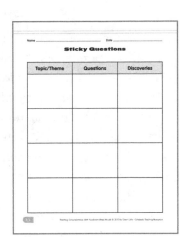

Sticky Questions, p. 70

## Session 1

**Activating Prior Knowledge:** This component is embedded in the lesson.

## Model Lesson

**Introduction:** To begin the lesson, explicitly state why it is important to activate prior knowledge. *Have you ever heard of the word* schema? *Schema refers to our background knowledge about a topic and our personal experience with that topic. We all bring our own personal schema to our reading. It is this schema that helps us understand what we read. We use our schema to make connections to what we read. By connecting what we already know about a topic to the new information we learn, we gain a better understanding of the text.*

**Conducting the Lesson:** *Today we are going to work on activating our prior knowledge. This means that we are going to learn a strategy that will help us connect information we already know about a topic—our schema—to the information we learn about the topic. Asking questions before we read helps us to make connections to the text. It gives us a purpose for our reading. In this case, our purpose is to find the answers to our questions.*

Then ask students what they already know about the topic. List responses on chart paper. Make sure to point out that each student will bring something different to the conversation based on his or her own unique experiences. Next, pass out one sticky note to each student. Ask students to write a question they have about the topic on it. As students complete their "sticky questions," they should place their sticky note on a second sheet of chart paper you've posted (this is just a holding place).

Show students the display copy of the Sticky Questions graphic organizer. Read each sticky note out loud and then have students sort the questions based on common themes/ threads. As students determine a new topic or theme, write it in the first column of the organizer and place the corresponding sticky note questions in the middle column. Then ask: *Do you think we'll find the answers to some of these questions in our reading?* After students respond, pose the following questions: *What if I said we weren't going to read the whole text? Do you think we could find the answers to some of our questions if we only read part of the text? Why? Why not?*

First, read aloud specific text features to see if information might be gleaned from these (i.e., captions, boxes, subheadings). Explain: *I am going to read aloud this article, but I am only going to read the text features. These include the headings, subheadings, captions, charts, and graphs. I may also skim and scan the text for bold or italicized words and read those aloud.*

As you read, think aloud when you come upon a text feature that may answer a question. Write the answer in the Discoveries column. After answering a few questions, ask: *How many of you have noticed that we've only answered a few of our questions? Do you think if we read the whole text we might be able to answer more of them? Why or why not?*

Read aloud the text. *I am going to read aloud the whole text. As I do, I am going to model how to locate the information that may answer our questions. Before reading, we activated our prior knowledge by asking questions we had about the topic. Now we are going to connect our prior knowledge with new information to help us understand the text.* As you read, stop to think aloud when you find an answer to one of the posted questions and write it on the display chart.

**Reflection:** Have pairs talk aloud about the strategy of activating prior knowledge by discussing one of the Essential Literacy Questions.

## Session 2

After the model lesson takes place, multiple guided practice sessions and individual student practice sessions should occur over a span of two weeks. In addition to the activities below, you may want to plan for extra activities based on your students' needs.

**Guided Practice:** Choose a text to read aloud to a group. Provide students with individual copies of the Sticky Questions graphic organizer. Have them write questions about the topic of the text on sticky notes. Ask them to organize their questions based on different topics. After you read aloud the text, tell students to write any discoveries they made.

**Student Practice:** Ask students to read a short piece of nonfiction text independently. Before students read, ask them to write several questions about the topic on individual sticky notes (use the small size to fit in notebooks). Then have students write their questions in the Sticky Questions graphic organizer. Using their questions as guides, they should create a series of topics. As students read, they should include the answers to the questions in the Discoveries column. This can be done with partners or independently.

## Beyond the Lesson

Before students write a report on a specific topic, have them complete sticky questions to activate their prior knowledge of the topic.

# Making the Connection

**McREL benchmark:** Uses prior knowledge and experience to understand and respond to new information

**Strategy:** Making connections (text to self, text to text, and text to world)

**Objective:** Students will be able to make connections to help them comprehend text.

## Essential Literacy Question (ELQ)

How does making personal connections to a text help you construct its meaning?

## Text Choices

◆ an autobiography (by the author of a text you may be reading in class)

◆ journal entries, such as material from *Covered Wagon Women: Diaries and Letters From the Western Trails (1840–1849)* by Kenneth L. Holmes and Anne M. Butler

◆ letters, such as material from *The Letters of John and Abigail Adams* by Frank Shuffelton

## Vocabulary Preview:

Conduct a Sentence Strip Vocabulary activity (see page 18) with students to determine the meaning of several words in context.

> ### Differentiation Tip
>
> Provide English language learners with a read aloud of a text that is related to their home country—for example, a short history of that country or a text about a holiday celebrated there. This activity gives students an opportunity to feel successful as they should have background knowledge of these topics and will be able to make more personal connections.

## Preparation

◆ Review a selected sample from your chosen text and use sticky notes to mark places where you will think aloud to make connections.

◆ Post the ELQ.

- Make two copies of the Making the Connection graphic organizer for each student and prepare a display copy.

- Gather the following materials: chart paper, marker, and sticky notes.

- Students will need their Reflect and Revise notebooks.

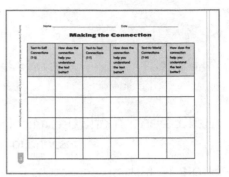

Making the Connection, p. 71

**Activating Prior Knowledge:** Provide students with three or four pieces of information from the text you selected. Ask if they can determine how the pieces of information relate to one other. Let them discuss with partners or in small groups. The goal is to see if students can figure out who or what the text is about and determine how making connections helped them.

## Model Lesson

**Introduction:** *Today, we are going to learn about making connections. When we make connections, we link something from the text to our own lives, to another text, or to the world around us. The connections we make to our own lives are called text-to-self connections. The connections we make to another text are called text-to-text connections, and the connections we make to the world are called text-to-world connections. By creating connections, we are activating our own schema and this helps us to better understand the text we're reading.*

*Now I am going to model what making connections looks like. As I read this text, I'm going to stop and think aloud when I come to a place where I can connect the text to my life, another text, or the world.* On the board or a piece of chart paper, write the codes students can use to note these connections: T-S (text-to-self), T-T (text-to-text), and T-W text-to-world).

**Conducting the Lesson:** Read aloud the piece of text, stopping to think aloud at the places you marked with sticky notes. You may say things like, *Hmm, I can make a text-to-self connection here* and then explicitly state what that connection is. For example, if you're reading a memoir, you may connect with the author's childhood in some way. As you continue reading, you may note a connection between the actual memoir and a fiction text the author has written. For this connection, you might say, *I can make a text-to-text connection* and then explicitly state what that connection is. Perhaps your class has read a story by the author, and in a memoir he or she describes something that happened in his or her childhood similar to an incident in the story. As you are making connections, be sure to think aloud about how the connection actually helps you better understand the text. Show students how you jot down some of your thoughts on sticky notes to help you remember the connections you made. Explain that the goal now is for them to learn how to make connections and to code these connections, but that eventually they should be able to make connections on their own without the use of sticky notes.

Exhibit the Making the Connection display chart you prepared. As you think aloud about the connections you made, fill in the appropriate columns on the chart, using your sticky notes.

**Reflection:** Have students use their Reflect and Revise notebooks to reflect on the strategy of making connections by answering the ELQ. Later on, students may want to revise their answers as they learn more about making connections.

## Session 2

After the model lesson takes place, multiple guided practice sessions and individual student practice sessions should occur over a span of two weeks. In addition to the activities below, you may want to plan for extra activities based on your students' needs.

**Guided Practice:** Encourage students in the group to use sticky notes to mark places in the selected text where they make connections. Then have them complete the Making the Connection organizer individually. Remember to encourage students to note how the connection helps them understand the text better.

**Student Practice:** Have students work independently to make connections in another part of the text that you read to them in the model lesson. Provide sticky notes for students to use when they make connections with that text. Give each student a copy of the Making the Connection graphic organizer and have them jot down their connections and the reasons the connections help them understand the text.

## Beyond the Lesson

1. Ask students to write character sketches or first-person narratives of the people they study in biographies, memoirs, or letters.

2. Have students compare their own lives to the lives of those they study in biographies.

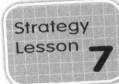

# The Wonderful World of Questions

**McREL benchmark:** Uses reading skills and strategies to understand a variety of informational texts

**Strategy:** Asking questions

**Objective:** Students will be able to determine questions he or she has before, during, and after reading and locate answers for them.

## Essential Literacy Question (ELQ)

How does asking questions help you understand the text you read?

## Text Choices

Most texts with photos or illustrations work well for this lesson. Possibilities include the following:

◆ a section of a trade book, such as *Volcanoes* by Lisa Magloff or *Spiders* by Kids Discover

◆ a newspaper or periodical article

## Vocabulary Preview:

Have students conduct a word splash (see page 18) to determine the meaning of words they will encounter in the text you are going to read aloud.

### Differentiation Tip

Make photocopies of the pictures from the text and show them to students, removed from context. Ask students what they think is going on in the pictures. Have them write questions they have about the pictures prior to hearing the read aloud. Discuss the pictures with students and clear up any misconceptions and answer any questions they have to help build their background knowledge.

## Preparation

◆ Review a piece of short text that has photos and/or illustrations and that lends itself to questioning.

◆ Post the ELQ.

◆ Make a copy of The Wonderful World of Questions graphic organizer for each student and prepare a display copy.

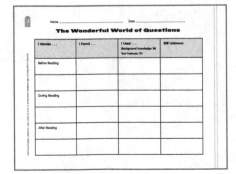

The Wonderful World of Questions, p. 72

◆   Students will need their Reflect and Revise notebooks.

**Activating Prior Knowledge:** This component is embedded in the lesson.

## Model Lesson

**Introduction:** Explicitly state why asking questions is important to our learning: *As humans, we are all naturally curious, and when we are curious, we ask questions. Sometimes when we read, we become confused about what we have read, or curious to learn more about the topic. At these times, we should stop and ask questions to clarify what it is we just read or to help us shape our understanding of the material. Asking questions is important to understanding anything, but asking questions is especially important when we read. If we teach ourselves to stop when we come to a point of confusion and ask questions, we will become better readers. Today, we are going to talk about questioning as a reading strategy. One way we can use this strategy is through a question chart.* Show the display copy of The Wonderful World of Questions graphic organizer you've prepared.

**Conducting the Lesson:** *Today, we are going to talk about how to ask and answer questions when we read. Until we learn to naturally ask questions on our own in our heads as we read, we are going to use The Wonderful World of Questions graphic organizer. This will help us to organize our questions into three categories: Before Reading, During Reading, and After Reading. Why do you think the organizer is broken into those three categories?* Allow time for students to respond and lead them to understand that good readers ask questions before, during, and after reading, if necessary.

Prior to reading aloud the chosen text, complete a feature walk and model how to list any before-reading questions you may have. *Before I read a nonfiction text, I always like to activate my background knowledge. One way to do this is to take a feature walk. This helps me to determine what the text may be about and also stimulates my mind to think of any questions I may have before I begin reading.* After modeling the feature walk (see page 19 for more information), say, *Now I'm going to write the questions I have on our chart under the Before Reading section of the I Wonder . . . column.* List any questions you have and discuss why you have questions about these particular items.

*Now I'm going to read the text. As I read, I may have questions that I wonder about. I may have questions that will help me clarify the text or I may just have questions regarding things I'm curious about. Either way, I'm going to write the questions in the During Reading section of the I Wonder . . . column.* As you read, stop and wonder aloud when you come to points of confusion and/or curiosity. Record your questions on the chart. When you've finished reading, explain that sometimes we're still left with questions when we come to the end of a text, although some of our earlier questions may have been answered. If you found the answers to any of your questions, record the answer in the I Found . . . column and its source in the I Used . . . column on the chart. If you did not find the answers to some of your questions, place a check mark in the Still Unknown column. *Now, I may still have questions after I've read a text. I'm going to write those questions in the After Reading . . . section of the I Wonder . . . column. I probably won't find answers to those questions in the text since I asked them after I finished reading However, you can use other resources to see if you can find the answers to your questions.*

**Reflection:** Have students form small groups and discuss how questioning before, during, and after reading may help them understand what they read. After allowing time for discussion, ask students to answer the ELQ in their Reflect and Revise notebooks. Remind students that they may want to revise their thinking as they continue to learn about asking questions.

## Session 2

After the model lesson takes place, multiple guided practice sessions and individual student practice sessions should occur over a span of two weeks. In addition to the activities below, you may want to plan for extra activities based on your students' needs.

**Guided Practice:** Help students ask questions before, during, and after reading when working in guided-reading groups. Provide individual copies of The Wonderful World of Questions graphic organizer for them to complete.

**Student Practice:** Partners can continue this lesson with another section of the same text or a completely different text. Encourage students to fill out The Wonderful World of Questions graphic organizer as they read together. After students have had enough practice using the organizer with partners, encourage them to use the organizer when they are reading on their own. Eventually, we want students to ask questions as they read, without the aid of the graphic organizer.

## Beyond the Lesson

As students conduct research in other subject areas, encourage them to use The Wonderful World of Questions organizer to list questions that arise. You can also encourage students to simply create I Wonder . . . questions about a topic and then conduct research to find the answers.

## Strategy Lesson 8 — Making Predictions

**McREL benchmark:** Uses prior knowledge and experience to understand and respond to new information

**Strategy:** Making predictions before and during reading to understand the text

**Objective:** Students will be able to use background knowledge to make predictions about what they read.

---

### Essential Literacy Questions (ELQs)

**1.** How does using background knowledge help you make predictions?

**2.** How does making predictions help you understand the text you read?

### Text Choices

◆ an article, such as "Safe Haven: Schoolkids, Scientists, and a President Join in the Fight to Protect Monarch Butterflies" by Emily Costello (*Science World*)

◆ a trade book, such as *Henry's Freedom Box* by Ellen Levine

### Vocabulary Preview:

Have students complete a Sentence Strip Vocabulary activity (see page 18) prior to reading the text. Write the sentences below on Sentence Strips.

◆ *These butterflies will never use their <u>overwintering</u> home again; they will breed and die up north.*

◆ *Now, <u>conservationists</u> are happy you'll help rebuild the butterflies' homes.*

> ### Differentiation Tip
>
> If students have a difficult time putting their predictions in writing, allow them to visualize their predictions. Then let students draw the information they predict will appear next.

## Preparation

◆ Review the text you will read aloud.

◆ Post the ELQs.

◆ Make a copy of the Prediction Squares graphic organizer for each student and prepare a display copy.

◆ Students will need their Reflect and Revise notebooks.

◆ Gather the following materials: a few sheets of chart paper, a marker.

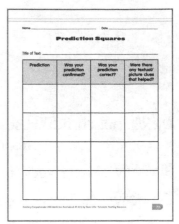

Prediction Squares, p. 73

## Session 1

**Activating Prior Knowledge:** Ask students what they already know about the topic of the text and explain that today you are going to read about that topic. *Before reading, we always want to activate our prior knowledge. Today, in order to activate our prior knowledge, we are going to create a collective list of what we already know.* Post a sheet of chart paper. List students' ideas about the topic. Once you have five to seven entries, ask students if they have any questions about the topic. *Okay, so we have listed several things we already know. Is there anything else we might want to know? Is there anything that we have questions about?* On another sheet of chart paper, list students' questions. Then ask students to answer the first ELQ in their Reflect and Revise notebooks: How does using background knowledge help you make predictions?

## Model Lesson

**Introduction:** Explicitly state what a prediction is and what the day's lesson is about. *Today, we are going to talk about making predictions. When we make predictions, we use our background knowledge to make a guess about what will happen in the text. Predictions are typically confirmed as we read further along in the text.*

**Conducting the Lesson:** Exhibit the Prediction Squares display chart. Explain that you are going to read aloud an article about the topic. *We have just activated our prior knowledge. As I read this article, I am going to make predictions about what information might appear next in the article. As I make these predictions, I'm going to post them in a prediction square. While I'm reading, I want you to quietly make predictions in your head: think about what information might appear next.*

Begin by reading the title of the article as well as the subtitle. If it's possible, state, *I'm going to make a prediction based on the title or the subtitle.* Write your prediction in the first square in the Prediction column. *As I read, I'll look for evidence that confirms my prediction.*

When you reach a place in the text that may confirm or deny your prediction, stop reading. Write whether the prediction was confirmed and note whether it was correct. Finally, record any textual or picture clues that helped confirm the prediction. Finish reading the article and continue to record your predictions, proof, and evidence in the chart. Ask students if any of the questions they had prior to reading were answered.

**Reflection:** Ask students to answer the second ELQ in a talk-aloud: How does making predictions help you understand the text you read?

## Session 2

After the model lesson takes place, multiple guided practice sessions and individual student practice sessions should occur over a span of two weeks. In addition to the activities below, you may want to plan for extra activities based on your students' needs.

**Guided Practice:** Have students use the Prediction Squares graphic organizer as they learn to make predictions in their guided-reading groups. Ask them to mark predictions that are confirmed with a "C." You can guide them into a lesson about inferences based on the predictions that are not confirmed (see Strategy Lesson 11, pages 52–51).

**Student Practice:** Give students independent opportunities to make predictions as they read. If students need to use the Prediction Squares graphic organizer, provide it, but if they have arrived at a point where they can make predictions independently, allow them to do so in their reading journals.

## Beyond the Lesson

Before teaching about a specific time period in history, choose a nonfiction trade book to read aloud or to have students read independently. To begin, ask students to make predictions based on the cover and title of the text. As you read aloud the text, or as students read it, ask them to continue to make predictions and note whether they are confirmed or not. Provide students with individual copies of the Prediction Squares graphic organizer to complete as needed.

# What Are the Important Ideas?

**McREL benchmark:** Uses text organizers to determine the main ideas and to locate information in a text

**Strategy:** Determining the important ideas in texts

**Objective:** Students will be able to use a graphic organizer to determine three important ideas from a text and defend their choices.

---

## Essential Literacy Questions (ELQs)

**1.** How does gleaning important information from a text help you understand it?

**2.** How does citing evidence from the text help you support your thinking?

## Text Choices

◆ a periodical article, such as "Delicate Balance" by Elena Cabral from *Scholastic News* or "Royal Reunion" by Michael E. Ruane and Fredrick Kunkle from *The Washington Post*

## Vocabulary Preview:

Have students complete a word splash (see page 18) prior to listening to the text.

### Preparation

◆ Review the text that you will read aloud.

◆ Post the ELQs.

◆ Make a copy of the What Are the Important Ideas? graphic organizer for each student and prepare a display copy.

### Differentiation Tip

Provide students with three pieces of evidence from the text and ask them to determine what they think the important idea is based on that evidence. Have them defend their choice.

What Are the Important Ideas, p. 74

- Students will need their Reflect and Revise notebooks.

- Gather the following materials: sticky notes and a marker.

## Session 1

**Activating Prior Knowledge:** Complete a feature walk of the text with your students (see page 19). Model how to read the subtitles, subheadings, and captions and list any questions you think might be answered by reading the article. Ask students to answer the first ELQ in their Reflect and Revise notebooks: How does gleaning important information from a text help you understand it? Discuss their responses.

## Model Lesson

**Introduction:** Present the display copy of the What Are the Important Ideas? graphic organizer and explicitly state what you will be doing today. *Our prior experience typically determines what we will take away when we read something. What I might think is an important idea of the text might not be as important to you. Today, we are going to find three important ideas from a text. But, we are also going to learn how to defend these ideas using evidence from the text.*

**Conducting the Lesson:** *We read the title and subtitle when we are activating our prior knowledge, so we have an idea of what we are going to read about.* After writing the title of the text on the graphic organizer, read the text. When you reach an important idea, stop and mark it with a sticky note. Continue reading and mark two more important ideas as you read. When you have finished reading, go back and point out the ideas that you deem important. Find evidence from the text that supports your thoughts and discuss how the idea and the evidence together helps you understand the text. Fill in the information on the display copy of the What Are the Important Ideas? graphic organizer.

*I have modeled how to determine three important ideas, find evidence from the text, and determine how it helps me understand the text. Do you think everyone in the class agreed with my choice of important ideas? Probably not and that's okay. We each determine the important ideas from the text ourselves and what you think is an important idea may not be the same to me. However, as long as we can support our important ideas with evidence from the text and can explain how it helps us understand the text, we are okay. Now, let's go back and look at the questions we asked when we were activating our prior knowledge. Determine if any of the questions can be answered.*

**Reflection:** Ask students to reflect on finding important ideas and write their thoughts in their Reflect and Revise notebooks. Have them answer the second ELQ in their notebooks and remind them that they may want to revise their answer as they continue to cite evidence from a text to support their thinking.

## Session 2

After the model lesson takes place, multiple guided practice sessions and individual student practice sessions should occur over a span of two weeks. In addition to the activities below, you may want to plan for extra activities based on your students' needs.

**Guided Practice**: Ask students to list three important ideas from a piece of text you are reading together. They should discuss and defend their main ideas with a partner. Provide students with individual copies of What Are the Important Ideas? graphic organizer to help guide their thinking.

**Student Practice:** After small groups of students read a short piece of text, ask them to complete the What Are the Important Ideas? graphic organizer to guide their thinking. Then tell them to write their three important ideas on a piece of paper and exchange them with their group members. As the papers rotate around the group, each member should read them and note whether he or she agrees or disagrees with the important ideas. Once the paper returns to the original student, the group should discuss the ideas they disagreed with.

## Beyond the Lesson

Teach students how to turn their list of important ideas into a written summary of the text. Explain to students that they should create a topic sentence based on their important ideas and then turn the important ideas into the details of the summary. Finally, tell students to create a concluding sentence. (For a lesson on summarizing, see Lesson 12 on pages 55–57.)

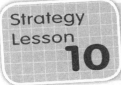

# Using the Five Senses to Visualize Text

**McREL benchmark:** Uses reading skills and strategies to understand a variety of informational texts

**Strategy:** Visualizing using sensory details

**Objective:** Students will be able to use sensory details to visualize information from the text.

## Essential Literacy Questions (ELQs)

**1.** How do sensory details help you visualize the text?

**2.** How does visualizing the text help you understand what you read?

## Text Choices

◆ an article or trade book with rich sensory details, such as *Into the Sea* by Brenda Z. Guiberson or *Journey of a Humpback Whale* by Caryn Jenner

## Differentiation Tip

Help students understand and make personal connections to text by reading aloud a visually stimulating text. Ask them to draw pictures of different aspects of the text that they visualize when you read aloud.

## Vocabulary Preview:

Complete a picture talk (see page 18) with your students prior to reading. Post pictures of vocabulary words from the text and guide students to an understanding of what the words mean.

## Preparation

◆ Find a text that is rich with sensory details. Read through it and mark areas where the author uses sensory details in a description.

◆ Post the ELQs.

◆ Make a copy of the Using the Five Senses to Visualize graphic organizer for each student and prepare a display copy.

◆ Students will need their reading journals and their Reflect and Revise notebooks.

Using the Five Senses to Visualize, p. 75

## Session 1

**Activating Prior Knowledge**: Have students record their background knowledge of the topic of the text in their reading journals. (If you're reading *Into the Sea*, the beach and zoo are two possible topics.) *Have you ever been to the _____? Take a minute to think about some of the sights, sounds, smells, textures, and tastes you remember. Create a list in your reading journal. If you haven't been to the _____, perhaps you have read about one or seen one on TV. Create a list of what you think you might see, hear, smell, feel, or taste at the _____.* Ask students to answer the first ELQ in their Reflect and Revise notebooks: How do sensory details help you visualize the text? Discuss their responses.

## Model Lesson

**Introduction:** *As humans, we use our five senses to help us figure things out every day. Sometimes, we don't even know we are using them. For example, when you open the refrigerator, you might smell something. Your brain processes the smell, and you realize that something has gone bad in the refrigerator. So, you have to look for the culprit. You didn't see what had gone bad at first, but your brain told you something smelled funny. As readers, we can use our senses to help us visualize what the author is describing. The author may describe a sound that we can "hear" as we read. Or perhaps, he or she describes a smell. Maybe you think you can actually smell it as you read. Whether the author is describing something we hear, smell, taste, see, or feel, we can use those details to help us visualize what is happening in the text. When we visualize, we make pictures in our minds. And when we can make pictures in our minds, we are able to understand the text better.*

*Today I am going to read a text in which the author took particular care to write with sensory details. I am not going to show you any pictures. Instead as I read, I am going to stop when I come across sensory details. I am going to think about what I hear, see, smell, taste, and feel and record that information on this graphic organizer. If I close my eyes, I might be able to visualize what is happening in the book using my five senses.*

**Conducting the Lesson:** Post the display chart of the Using the Five Senses to Visualize graphic organizer and begin reading *Into the Sea* or another text you've selected. As you read, stop to think aloud about the events that invoke your five senses and record them in the chart. Read about halfway through the text. With the help of the partially completed graphic organizer, draw a picture of something from the text that you visualized.

**Reflection:** Have students answer the second ELQ in their Reflect and Revise notebooks. As they learn more about sensory details and visualization, they may want to revise their thinking.

## Session 2

After the model lesson takes place, multiple guided practice sessions and individual student practice sessions should occur over a span of two weeks. In addition to the activities below, you may want to plan for extra activities based on your students' needs.

**Guided Practice:** Depending on the length of the text you used in the first session, you can continue the lesson in guided-reading groups with the same text or select another. Guide students to find sensory details in the remainder of the text or the new text that help them visualize what it is about.

**Student Practice:** Provide students with copies of the Using the Five Senses to Visualize graphic organizer. Have partners read a text together. Tell one student to read aloud several pages, while the other student visualizes what is happening and fills in the chart. Then have students switch roles, so that each student has a chance to visualize what is happening in the text and record it on his or her own chart. Each student should then draw a picture of one thing he or she visualized.

## Beyond the Lesson

1. Read aloud the chapter titled "East End" in *Knots in My Yo-Yo String* by Jerry Spinelli. Have students complete the Using the Five Senses to Visualize graphic organizer as they listen and determine how the author used sensory details to describe what was happening in the text.

2. Create a listening/learning center with a range of different texts. Provide an opportunity for students to record themselves reading aloud texts that invoke visualization and sensory images. Place the recordings in the center and allow students to listen to different recordings and draw a picture of what they visualize or have them complete the Using the Five Senses to Visualize organizer.

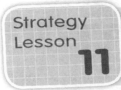

# Making Inferences

**McREL benchmark:** Draws conclusions and makes inferences based on explicit and implicit information in texts

**Strategy:** Making inferences

**Objective:** Students will be able to make inferences to help them comprehend text.

## Essential Literacy Questions (ELQs)

**1.** What are inferences?

**2.** How are inferences different from predictions?

**3.** How does making inferences help you better understand the text?

### Differentiation Tip

If it is difficult for students to put their inferences into words, ask them instead to draw a picture of what they think the text infers.

## Text Choices

◆ the text of a speech

◆ an essay

◆ preamble to the Declaration of Independence

◆ a trade book related to a historical time period, such as *Hana's Suitcase* by Karen Levine

## Vocabulary Preview:

Have students conduct a word splash (see page 18) to determine the meaning of words from the text.

## Preparation

◆ Review a piece of text that lends itself to making inferences.

◆ Post the ELQs.

◆ Make a copy of the Making Inferences graphic organizer for each student and prepare a display copy.

Making Inferences, p. 76

## Session 1

**Activating Prior Knowledge:** Reveal the topic of the text to students. Have them draw two pictures to demonstrate what they already know about this topic. Then ask students to list items related to the topic they want to learn more about. Finally, tell students to answer one of the ELQs in their Reflect and Revise notebook. Discuss their responses.

## Model Lesson

**Introduction:** To begin the lesson, discuss the difference between making predictions and inferring. *Today we are going to discuss making inferences. Making inferences is a little bit like being a detective. We have to use clues from the text to help us make an inference. When we infer, we use our background knowledge, combined with clues from the text or pictures, to make an educated guess about what is going to happen or about why something happened in the text. Making inferences is very similar to making predictions—but, when we predict, we make a guess about what is to come, instead of using background knowledge. In order to help us keep track of the inferences we make, we are going to use this graphic organizer.* Show the display copy of the Making Inferences graphic organizer.

**Conducting the Lesson:** Explain that as you read you will model how to use the facts from the text to make inferences about what the author is trying to tell you. *As I read, I'm going to stop when I come to something that might allow me to infer. It is easier for me to understand what I am trying to infer if I write down the fact from the text first.* Model with several facts, first writing the fact and then noting what you infer from it. For example, if your text is the preamble to the Declaration of Independence, you might write, "We hold these truths to be self-evident, that all men are created equal. . . ." and then note that you infer that the writer meant that the truth was clear—the American colonists had the right to create their own government and the King of England could not push them around anymore.

The bottom of the organizer contains a section for a photograph or an illustration from the text. Tell students that sometimes, they can make inferences from photographs or illustrations in the text. If there is a photograph in the text, state what is going on in it and then infer what you think it means. Record your observations.

**Reflection:** Have students answer another one of the ELQs in their Reflect and Revise notebooks.

## Session 2

After the model lesson takes place, multiple guided practice sessions and individual student practice sessions should occur over a span of two weeks. In addition to the activities below, you may want to plan for extra activities based on your students' needs.

**Guided Practice:** When you work with guided-reading groups, have students practice making inferences and then tell you how doing so helps them to better understand the text. Begin by reading a text with students. Ask group members to complete the Making Inferences graphic organizer.

**Student Practice:** Have students work in pairs. One partner draws a picture of something (could be the student's choice or something that happened in a text they read). The other partner tries to infer what is happening in the picture.

In another activity, have pairs use the Making Inferences graphic organizer as they read a text and make inferences based on what they've read.

## Beyond the Lesson

Create a literacy center that has high-interest newspaper and magazine articles. Have copies of the Making Inferences graphic organizer available at the center. Allow students to work in pairs and individually at the center to practice making inferences.

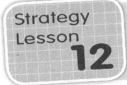

# Pulling It All Together: Summarizing Text

**McREL benchmark:** Summarizes and paraphrases information in texts

**Strategy:** Summarizing text

**Objective:** Students will be able to pull important pieces of information from a text to summarize the main ideas.

---

## Essential Literacy Questions (ELQs)

**1.** How can you determine what information is important in a text?

**2.** How can you pull information together to summarize a text?

**3.** How does summarizing help you better understand a text?

> ### Differentiation Tip
>
> Provide copies of the text for students so they can highlight or color code the pieces of information that will help them write a summary.

## Text Choices

◆ a section of a trade book, such as *Earthquakes* by Seymour Simon or *Kangaroos* by B. W. Brust

◆ a periodical or newspaper article

◆ a picture book autobiography, such as *A Picture Book of Harriet Tubman* by David Adler

## Vocabulary Preview:

Have students complete a Sentence Strip Vocabulary activity (see page 18) prior to reading the text.

## Preparation

◆ Review your chosen text. Determine ahead of time which information you think is important and what you want to be able to summarize from the text.

◆ Post the ELQs.

◆ Make a copy of the Pulling It All Together graphic organizer for each student and prepare a display copy.

◆ Students will need their Reflect and Revise notebooks.

◆ Gather the following materials: sticky notes and a marker.

Putting It All Together:
Summarizing Text, p. 77

## Session 1

**Activating Prior Knowledge:** Ask students to complete a K-W-L chart (see page 19) before you read aloud the text. Then have them answer one of the ELQs in their Reflect and Revise notebooks. Discuss their responses.

### Model Lesson

**Introduction:** Explain that one way we are able to understand what we read is by "pulling it all together." *When we read for information, our brains are working to understand what we read. Sometimes, in order to understand what we read, we need to pull several different pieces together. When we do this, we are summarizing the text. A summary helps us understand what the important points of a text are. If we are able to adequately summarize after reading a text, then we more than likely understood what we read. Today, we are going to use a graphic organizer to help us understand and "pull together" important pieces of information from the text we read.*

**Conducting the Lesson:** Show the display copy of the Pulling It All Together graphic organizer. *As I read, I am going to stop and write important pieces of information on sticky notes.* As you read and find important pieces of information in the text, write each one down on a sticky note. Place the sticky notes in a holding area. Once you have finished reading aloud and noting the important pieces of information, use the display copy of the graphic organizer to sort out your thoughts. Arrange the sticky notes by topic and write that topic under the Subtopics column on the organizer. Then, place the sticky notes in the Details From Text section for that topic. After reading and organizing the sticky notes on the graphic organizer, explain to students that you are now going to model how to take the information from the chart and write a summary of the text, and then do so. Explain that the summary should proceed in chronological order and should contain important

*Teaching Comprehension With Nonfiction Read Alouds*

pieces of information from the text. *Now I am going to show you how to write a summary from the information we have collected. Each subtopic will become one paragraph. I have to be sure to keep them in chronological order. The important information that I pulled from the text will become the details of the paragraph. So I'll turn a subtopic into a topic sentence, and then create sentences from the details on the sticky notes.* Also, emphasize that while you gathered a lot of information from the text, it is not necessary to use all of the pieces to write the summary; summaries are meant to be short and concise.

**Reflection:** Ask students to answer one of the ELQs in their Reflect and Revise notebooks. Remind them that they may revise their thoughts as they learn more about summarizing and as they become more comfortable with the process.

## Session 2

After the model lesson takes place, multiple guided practice sessions and individual student practice sessions should occur over a span of two weeks. In addition to the activities below, you may want to plan for extra activities based on your students' needs.

**Guided Practice:** In small groups, guide students to locate important pieces of information from a text. Provide students with copies of the Putting It All Together graphic organizer to organize their work. Help them write a summary pulling the important information from the graphic organizer and shaping it into a cohesive paragraph.

**Student Practice:** Pair students together and ask them to write a summary of one of the subtopics from the graphic organizer you created during Session 1. Next, have those students split up and work with a student who has summarized a different subtopic. They should read their summaries to each other. Continue until each student has heard a summary of all the subtopics.

## Beyond the Lesson

Have students write a summary of a text. Then ask them to work with a partner to see if the partner can work backward and fill out the Putting It All Together graphic organizer using the information from the summary.

# chapter 3

# Real-World Reading:
# Selecting Materials to Read Aloud

## Getting to Know Nonfiction Texts

Just as we need to become intimate with the fiction texts our students are reading for language arts, we must become familiar with a range of nonfiction texts. There are fiction texts you probably know inside out—either from years of teaching them or simply because you love reading them, or both. We must train ourselves to do the same with nonfiction.

How do we go about doing that? The great thing about nonfiction is that it is always around. Spend some time in the local library or bookstore. Ask the school librarian if he or she has any recommendations on the latest nonfiction texts that might work with your curriculum. Pore over children's magazines, newspapers, and trade books. Inquire about purchasing class subscriptions to a few of your favorite children's periodicals. Begin to read nonfiction with a critical eye. Search for various texts that can enhance your curriculum. Look for a variety of texts about a similar topic. Be on the lookout for different types of nonfiction; for example, when you travel, grab brochures at the local visitor's center.

When you stop to think about how much nonfiction we encounter on a daily basis, you'll realize it's a lot! We read the newspaper, billboards, mail, instructional manuals, and so on. Before we can effectively teach our students how to read nonfiction, we need to determine how *we* read nonfiction. Think about the strategies you use as you read a piece of nonfiction. If you are using specific strategies, then your students can use them, too. Acknowledging the strategies you use as a reader can help you plan nonfiction read alouds for your students.

Discussed below are different types of nonfiction that work well as read alouds. Each has its own place in the classroom and serves a different purpose. The key to keeping read alouds engaging and lively is to look beyond your traditional textbook to find suitable nonfiction texts that meet your needs.

## Trade Books

Trade books are typically books used as resources to supplement the curriculum. Reading aloud trade books can enrich content areas in many ways. Reading aloud a variety of trade books on a similar topic prior to studying that topic allows you to provide multiple perspectives. Trade books can be used to activate prior knowledge or build background knowledge before a new science, social studies, or math unit.

Prior to a new math unit, read aloud a portion of *Math on Call* (Kaplan, Debold, Rogalski, & Boudreau, 2004). This will help build students' background knowledge of the topic in a fun way. This book is bright and colorful and provides interesting information in call-outs. Read aloud a *Time for Kids* biography of a historical figure to tie into the time period you are studying. *National Geographic for Kids* has a line of books that appeal to kids and tie into many science topics (anatomy, life cycle, etc.)

## Big Books

We typically think of using big books in the primary classroom. They can have a place in the upper grades as well. The main benefit of big books in the primary classroom is that they're easy for all children to see as they gather around to listen to a read aloud. The same holds true for the upper grades. There are terrific nonfiction big books that can be used to teach reading strategies to the whole class. For instance, Newbridge has a great line of big books that older children find engaging and that ties into common science and social studies themes. In particular, big books are wonderful to use when teaching text features and text structures. As more publishers begin to see the need and use for big books in the upper grades, I hope we will start to see a larger variety of them.

## Newspapers

Newspapers are a rich source of nonfiction reading opportunities. They are excellent sources for finding science-related articles. If your grade or district studies local history, you can also typically find articles in your town or city newspaper about historical events or places. You can teach persuasive writing using letters to the editor as models. Analyze political cartoons and then create your own. And if you just want to model reading strategies for your students, current event topics in newspapers work beautifully.

## Magazines

There are so many fine children's magazines available now for our young readers—*Scholastic News, Time for Kids, National Geographic Kids, Ranger Rich*, just to name a few. These are good sources of nonfiction for several reasons. The articles are short. They deal with topics that are of interest to students. And the use of color and text features in the magazines pulls students in.

Local and regional magazines are also wonderful to read aloud to students. If your grade requirements include local history, check to see if a magazine is published for your city or state. If there is, more than likely it will contain engaging articles pertaining to the history of your region or state.

Another excellent source for interesting material is special edition magazines. Occasionally, magazine publishers like *U.S. News and World Report* will put out special editions on a single topic, such as the Civil War. Keep your eye out for these special editions, especially ones that relate to your curriculum.

## Miscellaneous Types of Nonfiction

Essays, speeches, brochures, letters to the editor, biographies, letters, diaries, directions, informational picture books, menus, informational posters, movie reviews, and book reviews can all be used effectively in the classroom. Each can be read aloud and used to teach important reading strategies.

## Organizing Nonfiction Texts

There are a variety of ways you can arrange your nonfiction texts. For instance, you can organize your consumable nonfiction pieces by curriculum points. As you find a magazine article or newspaper article that you want to use in your classroom, make a copy and add it to a binder. Separate the binder by curriculum or by strategy points. This way, you will have a running collection of nonfiction pieces to turn to when you need one.

You can use baskets to organize your nonfiction trade books. Group trade books by similar topics or by strategy lessons. Label an index card with the topic or strategy, laminate it, and punch two holes in it. Attach small rings through the holes and attach the card to the basket to easily locate a book by category.

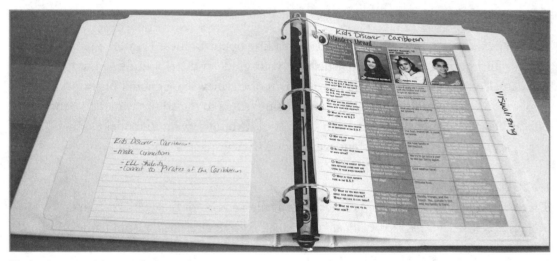

Binder for organizing nonfiction texts

# Choosing Nonfiction Texts

When choosing nonfiction texts to read aloud in the classroom, there are several things you should think about. What topic are you teaching? Do you have a specific strategy in mind? What type of text will work best for that topic and that strategy? As you begin to assemble a wide variety of nonfiction texts, think about what the topic of an accompanying lesson could be. Are you teaching a math lesson on geometry? Are you teaching a science lesson on rocks and minerals?

Creating a planning guide is helpful because it will enable you to locate the perfect nonfiction text that you need in order to successfully teach a lesson. You can use the Choosing Nonfiction Texts form as a planning guide. When you plan a lesson using a nonfiction text as a read aloud, determine the topic of your lesson first. This will make it easier to locate a text. Next, determine what type of text will best meet your needs. Are you working on making connections? You may want to use an autobiography or a diary entry. Are you working on text features? A big book may be your best bet because it is easy for everyone to see. Finally, note the strategies you want to model and whether you will need to activate prior knowledge and how to do it.

Choosing Nonfiction Texts, p. 78

# chapter 4

# Moving Beyond the Read Aloud:
# Assessment and Evaluation

As with all instruction, we should continually assess what we are doing and how our students are progressing. This provides us with data to determine our next instructional steps—which students need reinforcement and which students are prepared to move on. This opportunity aids us in our differentiation as well.

---

### Ways to Assess an Interactive Read Aloud

- ◆ Conferences

- ◆ Nonfiction Read-Aloud Comprehension Record

- ◆ Anecdotal Records

- ◆ Reflections

- ◆ Beyond the Lesson Activities

---

## Conferences

Conferences allow you to read one-on-one with a student and determine if he or she is able to apply the strategies you have taught. In addition, a conference is the fastest way to determine the likes and dislikes of a student. Knowing what kinds of texts a student likes to read enables you to pick books and articles that will make reading engaging and fun and motivate him or her to keep at it.

## Nonfiction Read-Aloud Comprehension Record

The Nonfiction Read-Aloud Comprehension Record (page 79) makes it easy to note which students comprehend a read aloud and specifically which strategies they are employing. There are nine strategies on the record. Students are not expected to use all of the strategies when discussing texts; instead, they may use one or two. Ahead of time, think of a question whose answer will provide the gist of the text. Use the Nonfiction Read-Aloud Comprehension Record to analyze student conversations when you offer the opportunity for a partner share. Observe how students discuss the text with one another; or examine the kinds of questions they ask or the connections they make.

**Note**: If you have parental permission, oftentimes it is easier to record discussions on audiotape. You can then go back and listen to the discussion at your leisure and carefully analyze and record strategies that students use.

## Nonfiction Read-Aloud Comprehension Record

Subject/Book Title ___Delicate Balance___

A. Uses organization and text structure to obtain meaning
B. Understands author's purpose for writing text
C. Remembers key events in sequential order
D. Recognizes cause and effect relationships
E. Makes connections to other selections read by comparing and contrasting texts to generate questions

F. Makes predictions before and during reading
G. Asks questions that generate discussion
H. Visualizes information from text to better understand text
I. Uses prior knowledge and information from the text to make inferences

| Student | A | B | C | D | E | F | G | H | I |
|---------|---|---|---|---|---|---|---|---|---|
| Susie | | | ✓ | | | | | ✓ | |
| Brian | ✓ | | ✓ | | | | | | |
| James | | | | ✓ | | | | | |
| | | | | | | | | | |
| | | | | | | | | | |
| | | | | | | | | | |
| | | | | | | | | | |

Sample of a Nonfiction Read-Aloud Comprehension Record

## Anecdotal Records

I use anecdotal records to keep track of specific student comments, thoughts, and opinions or to note specific reading behaviors. Using a manila file folder and color-coded index cards, I create my own set of anecdotal records for various literacy activities. They are easy to tote around and can be used when observing literature circles, for guided-reading lessons, or during a partner share following a read aloud. When creating an evaluation for a student, you can look back at your anecdotal records and note specific comments he or she made.

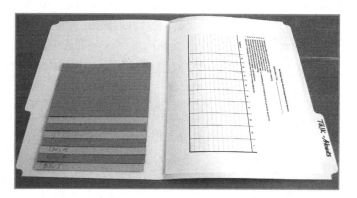

Anecdotal records

# Reflections

When students read independently, we typically have them reflect on their reading. This allows us to gain an inside look at their thinking, and research shows that reflection is necessary for students to fully comprehend written text. After conducting a read aloud, it is especially effective to have students reflect on what they heard. Doing so allows us to determine which students comprehended what was read. There are several ways we can have students reflect on their "reading."

**Talk-Alouds:** Providing an occasion for students to share with a partner can be a rich assessment opportunity. Just simply listening to what your students have to say in an informal setting allows you to learn what they already know or what needs to be reinforced. Use anecdotal records and the Nonfiction Read-Aloud Comprehension Record in tandem to record discussion among your students. The information you learn will help to determine your future instruction.

**Reflect and Revise Notebooks:** The Reflect and Revise notebook is a perfect way to determine if students are evaluating their own learning and synthesizing information they're receiving from various sources. I like to regularly ask students to reflect on the read aloud, either by answering an ELQ or in another fashion. You may want to have students reflect in their notebooks after they have completed a partner share as well. As students work with the strategy over the course of two weeks and in a variety of ways, always ask them to revise their thinking if it changes. Reflect and Revise notebooks are rich with information about students' understanding.

By using a Reflect and Revise notebook, we impart to students that when they've written their ideas down, it's possible to revise them as their own thinking evolves. Providing them the opportunity to share their thinking, yet to revise it as it changes is an important learning experience for them.

# Beyond the Lesson Activities

Beyond the Lesson activities are meant to extend student learning from the initial model read-aloud lesson to more of the same text or to different texts using the same strategy. Beyond the Lesson activities are a rich form of assessment because they enable you to see if students are able to transfer what they've learned to a different context. As you model strategy lessons through a read aloud, students are taking in what you teach them. Yet in order for them to truly internalize the strategy and begin to use it independently, they need plenty of chances to work with the strategy.

◆━━━■━━━■━━━◆

By using various forms of assessment, you can determine a fair evaluation of a student's reading abilities. Providing several assessment opportunities helps you create a more well-rounded evaluation of students. It is with this evaluation that we can determine if strategies are becoming an organic part of students' thinking. And we can use this information to shape our teaching and to clarify what students know and what they still need to learn.

# Nonfiction Read-Aloud
# Planning Sheet

Title of the Text: _____

Strategy:

_____

Essential Literacy Questions:

1. _____

2. _____

Ways to Model the Strategy:

_____

_____

Ways to Reflect:

_____

_____

Ways to Extend:

_____

_____

Ways to Assess:

_____

_____

Name _____ Date _____

# Structures of Text

| Cue Words | Text Structure | Title of Text |
|-----------|----------------|---------------|
|           |                |               |
|           |                |               |
|           |                |               |
|           |                |               |
|           |                |               |
|           |                |               |

Name _____ Date _____

# Nonfiction Text Features Checklist

Read a chapter or a section of your nonfiction text. Identify the text features. Then complete the checklist.

Title: _____

Author: _____ Chapter or section: _____

| Text Feature | Page Number | Purpose |
|---|---|---|
| Illustrations and Photographs | | |
| Illustrations | | |
| Photographs | | |
| Graphics | | |
| Diagrams | | |
| Charts | | |
| Maps | | |
| Tables | | |
| Graphs | | |
| Cue Words and Phrases | | |
| For example . . . | | |
| On the other hand . . . | | |
| But . . . | | |
| In conclusion . . . | | |
| For instance . . . | | |
| Therefore . . . | | |
| Most important . . . | | |
| In fact . . . | | |
| Text Organizers | | |
| Table of Contents | | |
| Index | | |
| Appendix | | |
| Glossary | | |
| Preface | | |
| Fonts and Effects | | |
| Heading | | |
| Bold face print | | |
| Italics | | |
| Color print | | |
| Labels | | |
| Captions | | |
| Titles | | |
| Bullets | | |

Name _____   Date _____

# What Is the Author's Purpose?

| Write to Inform | Write to Persuade | Write to Entertain |
|---|---|---|
| | | |
| | | |
| | | |
| | | |

Name _____

Date _____

# Inferring Vocabulary

| Word | Inferred Meaning | How Do I Know? (clues from text) | Sentence From Text | Actual Definition (determine from text or dictionary) | Was My Inference Close? |
|------|-----------------|----------------------------------|--------------------|-------------------------------------------------------|-------------------------|
|      |                 |                                  |                    |                                                       |                         |
|      |                 |                                  |                    |                                                       |                         |
|      |                 |                                  |                    |                                                       |                         |
|      |                 |                                  |                    |                                                       |                         |

Name _____     Date _____

# Sticky Questions

| Topic/Theme | Questions | Discoveries |
| --- | --- | --- |
|  |  |  |
|  |  |  |
|  |  |  |
|  |  |  |

Name _____

Date _____

# Making the Connection

| Text-to-Self Connections (T-S) | How does the connection help you understand the text better? | Text-to-Text Connections (T-T) | How does the connection help you understand the text better? | Text-to-World Connections (T-W) | How does the connection help you understand the text better? |
|---|---|---|---|---|---|
|  |  |  |  |  |  |
|  |  |  |  |  |  |
|  |  |  |  |  |  |
|  |  |  |  |  |  |

Name _____

Date _____

# The Wonderful World of Questions

| I Wonder . . . | I Found . . . | I Used . . .<br>(Background Knowledge: BK<br>Text Features: TF) | Still Unknown |
| --- | --- | --- | --- |
| Before Reading | | | |
| During Reading | | | |
| After Reading | | | |

*Teaching Comprehension With Nonfiction Read Alouds* © 2010 by Dawn Little • Scholastic Teaching Resources

Name _____  Date _____

# Prediction Squares

Title of Text: _____

| Prediction | Was your prediction confirmed? | Was your prediction correct? | Were there any textual/ picture clues that helped? |
|---|---|---|---|
|  |  |  |  |
|  |  |  |  |
|  |  |  |  |
|  |  |  |  |

Name _____    Date _____

# **What Are the Important Ideas?**

Title of Text: _____

Important Idea #1: _____

_____

Evidence from the text: _____

_____

How it helps me understand the text: _____

_____

Important Idea #2: _____

_____

Evidence from the text: _____

_____

How it helps me understand the text: _____

_____

Important Idea #3: _____

_____

Evidence from the text: _____

_____

How it helps me understand the text: _____

_____

Name _____     Date _____

# Using the Five Senses to Visualize

When I heard/read _____,

I used my five senses to help me visualize the text.

| Page | I heard . . . | I saw . . . | I felt . . . | I smelled . . . | I tasted . . . |
|------|---------------|-------------|--------------|-----------------|----------------|
|      |               |             |              |                 |                |

Use the sensory details to visualize what you think is happening in the text.
Draw a picture.

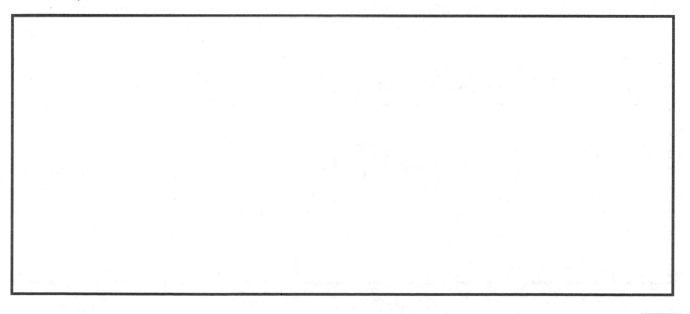

Name _____  Date _____

# Making Inferences

| Facts | Inferences |
|-------|------------|
|       |            |
|       |            |
|       |            |
|       |            |
|       |            |

(What does the text actually say?)   (What can we interpret from the text?)

| Pictures From the Text | Inferences |
|------------------------|------------|
|                        |            |

Name _____ Date _____

# **Pulling It All Together:**
# **Summarizing Text**

Title of Text: _____

| Subtopics | Details From Text |
|-----------|-------------------|
|           |                   |
|           |                   |
|           |                   |
|           |                   |

Adapted from Harvey & Goudvis (2007)

# Choosing Nonfiction Texts

**Topic of the Lesson:** _____

**Curriculum Match** (circle):

Language Arts          Science          Social Studies          Math

**Type of Text** (circle):

Big Book          Trade Book          Magazine          Newspaper

Other: _____

**Title of the Text:** _____

**Possible Strategy Lessons:**

**Ways to Activate Prior Knowledge:**

# Nonfiction Read-Aloud Comprehension Record

## Subject/Book Title _____

A. Uses organization and text structure to obtain meaning
B. Understands author's purpose for writing text
C. Remembers key events in sequential order
D. Recognizes cause and effect relationships
E. Makes connections to other selections read by comparing and contrasting texts to generate questions

F. Makes predictions before and during reading
G. Asks questions that generate discussion
H. Visualizes information from text to better understand text
I. Uses prior knowledge and information from the text to make inferences

| Student | A | B | C | D | E | F | G | H | I |
|---------|---|---|---|---|---|---|---|---|---|
|  |  |  |  |  |  |  |  |  |  |
|  |  |  |  |  |  |  |  |  |  |
|  |  |  |  |  |  |  |  |  |  |
|  |  |  |  |  |  |  |  |  |  |
|  |  |  |  |  |  |  |  |  |  |
|  |  |  |  |  |  |  |  |  |  |
|  |  |  |  |  |  |  |  |  |  |
|  |  |  |  |  |  |  |  |  |  |
|  |  |  |  |  |  |  |  |  |  |
|  |  |  |  |  |  |  |  |  |  |

# Professional Sources Cited

Anderson, R. C., Hiebert, H. H., Scott, J. A., & Wilkinson, I. A. G. (1985). *Becoming a nation of readers: The report of the commission on reading.* Washington, D.C.: National Institute of Education.

Davey, B. (1983). Thinking aloud: Modeling the cognitive processes of reading comprehension. *Journal of Reading, 27,* 44–47.

Fountas, I. C., & Pinnell, G. S. (2005). *Teaching for comprehending and fluency, K–8: Thinking, talking, and writing about reading.* Portsmouth, NH: Heinemann.

Harvey, S. (1998). *Nonfiction matters: Reading, writing, and research in grades 3–8.* Portland, ME: Stenhouse.

Harvey, S., & Goudvis, A. (2007). *Strategies that work* (2nd ed.). Portland, ME: Stenhouse.

Kaplan, A., Debold, C., Rogalski, S., & Boudreau, P. (2004). *Math on call.* Wilmington, MA: Great Source.

Ketch, A. (2005). Conversation: The comprehension connection. *The Reading Teacher, 59(1),* 8–13.

Mid-continent Research for Education and Learning, www.mcrel.org, retrieved October 7, 2007.

Ogle, D. (1986). "K-W-L: A teaching model that develops active reading of expository text." *The Reading Teacher 39,* 564–570.

Ray, K. W. (1999). *Wondrous words.* Urbana, IL: National Council of Teachers of English.

Sharer, P. L., Pinnell, G. S., Lyons, C., & Fountas, I. (2005). Becoming engaged readers. *Educational Leadership, 63,* 24–29.

Smith, F. (1978). *Reading without nonsense.* New York: Teachers College Press.

Snowball, D. (1995). Building literacy skills through nonfiction. *Teaching K–8, 25,* 62–63.

Trelease, J. (1982). *The reading handbook.* New York: Penguin.

# Children's Literature Cited

Adler, D.A. (1992). *A picture book of Harriet Tubman.* New York: Holiday House.

Bach, J. S. ( 2004). *Bicycling.* North Mankato, MN: Smart Apple Media.

Berger, M. (1995). *Animal senses.* New York: Newbridge.

Bjerklie, D. (2006). *Butterflies.* New York: HarperCollins.

Brust, B.W. (1999). *Kangaroo.* Poway, CA: Wildlife Education, Ltd.

Cabral, E. (2007). Delicate balance. *Scholastic News.* 4–5.

Costello, E. (2008). Safe haven. *Science World.* 8–11.

Edwards, R. (2005). *Who was Leonardo da Vinci?* New York: Grossett and Dunlap.

Giesecke, E. (2003). *From seashells to smart cards.* Chicago: Reed Educational and Professional Publishing.

Guiberson, B. Z. (2000). *Into the sea.* New York: Holt.

Gutman, B. (2005). *Lance Armstrong: A biography.* New York: Simon Pulse.

Hakim, J. (2005). *A history of US: The new nation.* New York: Oxford University Press.

Holmes, K. L. & Butler, A. M. (1995). *Covered wagon women, volume 1: Diaries and letters from the western trails, 1840–1849.* Lincoln, NE: University of Nebraska Press.

Iasevoli, B. (2009). Remembering Lincoln. *Time for Kids.*

Jenner, C. (2002). *Journey of a humpback whale.* New York: DK Publishing.

Krull, K. ( 2002). *Lives of the musicians: Good times, bad times (and what the neighbors thought).* New York: Harcourt.

Levine, E. (2007). *Henry's freedom box.* NY: Scholastic.

Levine, K. (2002). *Hana's suitcase.* Chicago: Albert Whitman & Company

Levine, R. (2000). *Story of the orchestra: Listen while you learn about the instruments, the music, and the composers who wrote the music!* New York: Black Dog and Leventhal.

Magloff, L. (2003). *Volcanoes.* New York: DK Publishing.

Nagda, A. W., & Bickel, C. (2002). *Chimp math: Learning about time from a baby chimpanzee.* New York: Henry Holt.

Naylor, P. R. (2001). *How I came to be a writer.* New York: Aladdin.

Naylor, P. R. (2000). *Shiloh.* New York: Aladdin.

*Ranger Rick.* Washington, D.C.: National Wildlife Federation.

Rylant, C. (1982). *When I was young in the mountains.* New York: Dutton Children's Books.

Ruane, M. E., & Kunkle, F. (2007). Royal reunion. *Washington Post.*

Sachar, L. (2000). *Holes.* New York: Scholastic.

Shuffelton, F. (2003). *The letters of John and Abigail Adams.* New York: Penguin.

Simon, S. (1991). *Earthquakes.* New York: HarperCollins.

*Spiders.* (2003). New York: Kids Discover.

Spinelli, J. (1998). *Knots in my yo-yo string.* New York: Knopf.

*Secrets of the Civil War.* (2008). Washington, D.C.: U.S. News and World Report.